LOOK, SPEAK, & BEHAVE™

For Women

LOOK, SPEAK, & BEHAVE™
For Women

Expert Advice on Image,
Etiquette, and Effective
Communication
for the Professional

Jamie Yasko-Mangum, C.I.C.

Skyhorse Publishing

www.skyhorsepublishing.com

10 9 8 7 6 5 4 3 2 1

All photographs © Steve Strobl

Library of Congress Cataloging-in-Publication Data

Yasko-Mangum, Jamie.
  Look, speak, & behave for women : expert advice on image, etiquette, and effective communication for the professional / Jamie Yasko-Mangum.
      p. cm.
  Includes bibliographical references and index.
  ISBN-13: 978-1-60239-026-3 (hardcover : alk. paper)
  ISBN-10: 1-60239-026-6 (hardcover : alk. paper)   1. Success in business.
2. Self-presentation. 3. Women's clothing. 4. Business communication.
I. Title. II. Title: Look, speak, and behave for women.

HF5386.Y345 2007
395.5'2082--dc22

                                        2007000997

Printed in the United States of America

Table of Contents

Table of Contents

ELEMENT TWO: A POLISHED APPEARANCE

Table of Contents

Table of Contents

Table of Contents

Acknowledgments

*L*ook, Speak, & Behave™ for Women could not have been written without the love and support of my husband, Kevin, and my two wonderful boys, Stone and Spencer. I truly appreciate your patience, encouragement, and understanding more than you all know! I want to deeply thank my parents, who are my role models and have always believed in me and given me unconditional support. I also appreciate all encouragement from my extended family and friends. To my friends, thank you for your patience; what troopers!

Thank you to my assistant, Jennifer, for all her hard work. And thank you to my personal and corporate clients who encouraged me in writing this book. All of you were an integral part of this venture. I want to thank Steve Strobl for his spectacular photography and patience. Thank you to my classy friends and clients— Amy, Jennifer, Elizabeth, Georgiana, Brenda, and Melissa—who modeled for this book.

A big thank you to Steve, who introduced me to Tony at Skyhorse Publishing. I want to thank Tony and Bill for their guidance, patience, and support in my writing. Also thank you to the rest of the team at Skyhorse Publishing.

Finally, but most importantly, I want to thank God for giving me strength and perseverance in this writing venture and for making me able to write about what I love to teach.

—Jamie Yasko-Mangum
December 2006

Introduction

*D*o you project a credible and respectable self-image? Whether you are a recent college graduate, a junior professional, working from home, or a seasoned professional, it is important to understand the ways in which your self-image affects your journey to becoming and staying a successful female professional. Whatever your age, profession, or position is, you have the ability to control and mold your self-image to project your self-worth, credibility, authority, and reputation. In *Look, Speak, & Behave™ For Women*, I help you to do just that. I introduce you to my self-image building block system for the female professional. The self-image building block system unites your inner and outer images. The key to success is uniting your identity (your age, profession, and position) with all four self-image elements. The elements are:

One   Positive Self-Esteem
Two   A Polished Appearance
Three Speaking Intelligently
Four   Behaving with Pride

In the Positive Self-Esteem section, you'll learn how to build your self-confidence so you can motivate yourself. In the Polished Appearance section, you'll learn why your appearance matters both on and off the job. You'll also learn how to dress with a style that is comfortable, polished, and age-appropriate, that projects confidence in any situation, and that saves money, through my Outfit Option™ Work Wardrobe. In the Speaking Intelligently section, you will develop communication skills to help you speak, listen, and communicate effectively in a variety of work situations. Finally, in the Behaving with Pride section, you will learn how to exude and command respect. Within each chapter, I give you real-world information, exercises, examples, and photos. Each of these traits builds upon the other, creating a system that helps you to mold and enhance your self-image and will help you reach your desired results.

I have taught many women to be successful business professionals, and now I will teach you too. Remember: the care you invest in yourself reflects the care you invest in your career. You never know who may be looking at you or whom you may meet!

CHAPTER ONE

What Does Your Mirror Say?

*L*adies, when you look at yourselves in the mirror, what do you see? Do you value who you are and, more importantly, where you are in your professional life? Many women have hectic schedules and don't take the time to evaluate who they really are. A mirror reflects both how you feel inside and how you look outside. A woman's image is not just about her inner or outer self, but rather a combination of both working together.

In the business world, no matter your age, profession, or position, your individual image reflects who you are, first to yourself, then to your employees or employers, colleagues, clients, and potential clients. Your image must reflect *self-worth*. Self-worth does not mean how much money you make in your job, but how much you care about yourself. Self-worth is critically important! When you positively reflect self-worth, you increase your opportunity for professional success. Without self-worth, you can feel complacent, timid, egotistical, paranoid, jealous, and spiteful, which can lead to distrust and disappointment in the workplace, carelessness, unreliability, and, potentially, disaster.

Your journey to self-worth and professional success begins here. Throughout this book, I'll refer to generation (age), profession, and position. These three dynamics identify where you are in your life. It's crucial for all women to understand these self-identifiers so that they can build their professional success on their true selves.

AGE GROUP/GENERATION

Today's workforce is made up of four diverse generations. Within those generations, there are many different personalities. In *When Generations Collide*, Linda C. Lancaster and David Stillman define the generations according to birth years as follows:

- WWII (1900–1945)
- Baby Boomer (1946–1964)
- Generation X (1965–1980)
- Generation Y or Millennial (1981–1999)

The two largest generations are the Baby Boomers (eighty million members) and Generation Y or Millennial (seventy-six million members). Many researchers, including Lancaster and Stillman, offer their own labels for each generation; however, I do not think you can completely label everyone within the same generation. While you may be a WWII, Baby Boomer, Generation

X, or Generation Y woman, you may also share some attributes with women of other generations, along with your own thoughts, attitudes, decorum, and beliefs.

Problems in the workplace often arise when generations have conflicts about issues such as dress attire, organizational development, dedication, judgments, behavior, open mindedness, etc. A helpful way to avoid these conflicts is to understand the general attributes of each generation. Let's look at a few.

- **WWII** professional women are enjoying retirement or changing career paths to pursue occupations or hobbies that they love. They are disciplined, loyal, dedicated, detail-oriented, and hard workers.
- **Baby Boomers** are in executive and managerial level positions, or in the midst of changing careers. These women exemplify feminism, dedication, strong work habits, optimism, and loyalty.

- **Generation X** professional women can be found in a wide variety of professional positions, from managers to entrepreneurs. They are independent, confident, open-minded, optimistic, family-oriented, and modern.
- **Generation Y or Millennial** professional women are just graduating from college and beginning to pursue their careers. They are entrepreneurial, free-spirited, independent, dedicated to their specializations, and technologically savvy.

As you can see, while there are some similarities among the generations, there are also clear differences. Each generation can learn from the others, sharing ideas, inspiration, solutions, experience, and wisdom. Judgment, elitism, disrespect, arrogance, rudeness, and pretentiousness have no place in the workplace.

The corporate world has changed positively for women over the decades. Today, there are many more career opportunities for women than there once were. While women continue to struggle for equality in some positions and occupations, there has been a vast improvement, and there will be more improvement as the workplace continues to evolve.

WHERE ARE YOU IN YOUR PROFESSION?

Do you know where you are in your profession? You may be facing a career choice, advancing, setting off on an entrepreneurial venture, or re-entering the workplace after time away. To help you understand where you are and where you want to go, you should conduct a professional self-inventory. Below are some questions to ask yourself; you may want to write your answers on a separate piece of paper.

Professional Self-Inventory

- Are you a college student embarking on your first professional job?

What Does Your Mirror Say?

- Are you ready to make the transition back to the workforce after staying home with your children?
- Are you unsettled with your current field of work?
- Do you "job hop"?
- Are you in a supervisory position, but unable to unite the team?
- Are you often reprimanded?
- Are you starting your own small business?
- Do you lack respect from your employees despite your executive position?
- Do you feel taken for granted?
- Are you changing careers?
- Do you feel your age is a hindrance?
- Do you feel a lack of respect at work?
- Are you unproductive, lazy, or not driven?
- Are you overlooked?

Is your answer to any of these questions "yes"? Ask yourself why you feel this way and how you can improve yourself. I recommend setting goals for improvement. A goal is achievement-oriented and requires you to exert more effort than you normally might. Goals are not meant to remain sedentary on a piece of paper; they are meant to be focused on and accomplished. Focusing on a goal means visualizing the plan you are going to use to achieve it and putting that plan into action.

Visualization is one tool you can use to attain a goal. Think of ways to attain your goal that, while realistic, make you reach beyond your current situation. When you find an approach that could be productive, run it through your mind step by step and imagine yourself reaching your goal. Replaying this plan in your mind will give you the willpower to put it into action and achieve it.

You should always have an outline of both short-term and long-term goals. Short-term goals lead to long-term accomplishments. This can be a difficult process at times, but discipline and perseverance will help you reach your goals and enhance your level of professional success.

WHAT IS YOUR POSITION?

It's nice for me to observe that elitism is decreasing in the workplace. I have witnessed great gains in various organizations when the entire workforce worked together regardless of title or level of employment. When I first began my professional life, elitism was rampant. At least two of my managers or bosses boldfaced or capitalized their titles on paper to ensure that everybody was aware of their positions. Not a good way to manage. *Leaders need to unite, not separate.* I will talk more about leaders later in this chapter.

If you are in a support, clerical, industrial, administrative, managerial, or executive-level position, it is important to understand that you are a team player first. A team player pitches in and does not boast, lack motivation, say "It's not my job," or take full credit for things others have done. A team player synergizes with others by valuing differences, having an open mind, finding new ways to do things, showing initiative, pitching in even though it is not her job, encouraging, and sharing credit.

If you are in a leadership position or if your goal is to become a leader, you not only need to be a team player, but you must also be self-motivated, confident, inspirational, excellent at communicating, mature, and achievement-oriented. You must be an active listener, a group motivator, and a hard worker who shares credit.

Your attitude at work sends vibes through the organization, and they should be positive. You should be a talent within your organization, helping it to run smoothly. When you do not care about your position and show laziness, entitlement, a sloppy appearance, lack of appreciation for staff, or unreliability, you

erode your career and possibly your organization. You may think that you do not show
these symptoms, but to be sure, ask a trusted
colleague or a sincere family member. At work,
you need to be productive and challenged. If
you are not, it is time to reevaluate your position and determine where you want to be.

You know and understand the three factors
that make up your identity: generation, profession, and position. Now you need to recognize,
acknowledge, and apply those factors to the
four self-image traits so that you feel in control,
and on the path to becoming a professional
success. I will define terms, outline processes,
and give examples that you can realistically follow. It is up to you to care enough about yourself to create confidence and become a success;
it takes personal responsibility. Again, the four
self-image elements are:

One   Positive Self-Esteem
Two   A Polished Appearance

Three Speaking Intelligently
Four Behaving with Pride

You will need to connect these self-image elements with your age, profession, and position. The way you care about yourself reflects the way you care about other aspects of your life. If you feel bad, look sloppy, speak crudely, or act rudely, you will doom your chance for professional success. Don't let that happen to you—possess self-worth!

ELEMENT ONE

Positive Self-Esteem

CHAPTER TWO

Positive Self-Esteem

*W*hat is self-esteem? Today, every psychologist, psychiatrist, or family therapist has a label for it or a theory about it. I believe excellent self-esteem involves:

- Believing in yourself
- Being honest
- Being responsible
- Aspiring to greater things
- Inspiring
- Accepting differences

- Respecting yourself and others
- Validating others

You must possess positive self-esteem in every aspect of your life; it is the foundation of your identity. See Box 1.

Box 1
Professional and
Personal Balance

Women, especially women from the later WWII and early Generation X generations, often put their careers before their personal lives. They may skip vacations, forgo their interests and hobbies, put off getting married and having children, or lose touch with family. Their careers come first.

I know this happened to me. I did not want to get married straight out of college, did not want children until I was 30, and often neglected personal relationships because of my career.

Having a strong career drive is obviously key to professional success, but it can be toxic if not handled with care. It can unravel your accomplishments and leave you lonely. You must appreciate the importance of your personal life, because without it, there is no value to your professional life.

You need family and friends who love you unconditionally, support you, and inspire you, and you should do the same for them. This two-way support will increase your self-esteem and benefit everyone around you.

You also need time for self-renewal. Find a favorite location or activity that relaxes you and "recharges your batteries." Take time to be alone. This time can be hard to schedule, but even five minutes can make a difference.

Balancing your personal and professional lives can be challenging, but when you acknowledge the value of both, you will be happier and more successful.

Today, I have a wonderful husband, two spectacular kids, and a great network of family and friends. I make a concerted effort to balance my first priority, my family, with my career.

Are you ready to look at your self-esteem? In order to build it up, first you need to see if you are bringing yourself down.

SIGNS OF LOW SELF-ESTEEM

- You think about yourself often and analyze why you are the way you are.

- You fear adversity and may be alienated from or in opposition to parents and authority figures.
- You do not smile easily. You hold pessimistic views.
- You are unwilling or unable to set and achieve your goals.
- You keep to yourself and prefer being alone.
- You avoid eye contact and find it difficult to genuinely trust others.
- You don't take risks.
- You are difficult to be around. You are antisocial or even violent.
- You talk to yourself negatively, you do not tell the truth or keep your word, and you do not forgive yourself or others. You may lack empathy, compassion, and remorse.

Raising your self-esteem requires changes in negative beliefs and timid or inappropriate behavior. If your self-esteem is low, you must start believing in yourself and proactively taking possession of your life. When you practice positive thinking, you will experience personal and professional success.

Let's look more closely at the attributes of self-esteem. This is the time to invest in yourself. Remember: your positive self-esteem is the foundation of your identity.

BELIEF IN YOURSELF

The most important part of self-esteem is belief in yourself. Do you remember your first day of school, or your first day of work? You were probably anxious, maybe even a little scared. Embarking on a new opportunity or venture is scary, no doubt about it! But you must possess internal strength. Believing in yourself requires discipline, realization, and perseverance. Discipline involves replacing negative thoughts with positive ones; realization is visualizing your opportunity or venture; and perseverance is commitment, even in tough times. A little hesitation is normal, but if you believe in yourself, you can achieve great success.

HONESTY

Honesty is being truthful to yourself and others. Too often, people act different ways around different people instead of being their genuine selves. Honesty within yourself gives you confidence and shows others that they can have confidence in you too. If you are dishonest, co-workers will not include you in their collaboration; clients will leave; potential clients become scarce; your employer terminates you; or your business fails.

You may think that lying or being deceitful is harmless because it gets you a promotion or hooks a client. But lying not only makes you a deceitful person, it can lead you to professional disaster—just pick up a newspaper and you'll see what can happen to employees with unethical business practices. Honesty is always the best policy!

RESPONSIBILITY

Responsibility means being accountable for your actions. You are responsible for all of the choices you make. In the corporate world, you must assume resumé responsibility (not lying about your qualifications), budget responsibility (not stealing), and job responsibility (not making excuses). When you make the wrong choices, you are usually the one who pays the consequences. Make right choices at work and promote corporate responsibility, whether you are a small business owner or a multi-million-dollar conglomerate.

ASPIRING TO GREATER THINGS

Aspiring is bettering yourself. It takes motivation and hard work. You are not entitled to anything;

you must work for it. Self-motivation demands discipline, exertion, and initiative. You are no longer a child who needs to be told what to do. If your job requires multiple job responsibilities and you do not know how to do some of them, ask for instruction—this shows self-motivation. If your lack of formal education prevents you from advancing professionally, take classes. If you are a leader in your organization, do not shirk your responsibility; lead by example.

INSPIRING OTHERS

People are often reluctant to mentor co-workers because they worry that those co-workers will use their advice to supersede them. Hogwash! When you feel paranoid, you can't succeed in aspiring to greater things. But when you let go of paranoia and share your knowledge, you maximize your employees' and colleagues' potential, helping not only them, but also your organization and, by extension, yourself.

ACCEPTING DIFFERENCES

Everyone is different. Criticizing others for their opinions, beliefs, and ways of doing things is not constructive, and it indicates negativity and lack of respect. You will often work with people with whom you do not agree. Unless you are morally against their beliefs (in which case you should express your opinion), you need to learn to "agree to disagree." For example, if you have a disagreement with a colleague about the proper way to do something, agree to disagree until you've learned the correct procedure. When you learn to accept differences, your professional and personal lives will be smoother.

RESPECTING YOURSELF AND OTHERS

Do you respect yourself and others? Take a few moments to reflect. Respectful people behave unselfishly, accept diversity, avoid hurtful remarks, and display kindness and self-control. In the behavior chapter, I will spend more time on this subject; for now, remember that respect is earned, not given.

VALIDATING OTHERS

One example of validation is praising someone who has gone above and beyond his or her job responsibilities. You need to give validation and you need to receive it, because validation promotes high morale and productivity. Praise can come from leaders in organizations, co-workers, customers, clients, patients, or anyone else. When you show initiative with your job responsibilities, provide exceptional customer service, or help co-workers, hopefully you will receive acknowledgment and praise. I realize that there are some people within organizations who do not validate others—that's unacceptable, so don't let that person be you! See Box 2.

Box 2
Do You Praise
Or Take For Granted?

When you were a child, your mom, dad, or caretaker clapped for you when you took your first step, hugged you when your heart was broken, told you they were proud of you when you graduated from college, and so on. When you receive encouragement, you feel good and more confident about your life's challenges.

Now that you are a working adult, it is your responsibility to give encouragement and praise when someone has gone above and beyond his or her job responsibility or has given a stellar performance.

Do you validate when . . .

- A co-worker helps with a project that turns out to be a success?

- An employee puts in extra hours without being told to?
- An employee makes a customer or client feel extra-special?
- A co-worker volunteers to do the shift you were supposed to work?
- Your employee betters him or herself?

When you validate others, you show that you appreciate them and that they are an important part of the organization. If you don't validate others, start!

Now you have read about self-esteem and what you need to do to build your self-confidence. Practice positive thinking and believing every day. Your challenges and hurdles will become opportunities!

Let's turn to the second self-image element, "A Polished Appearance," and continue your journey to professional success.

ELEMENT TWO

A Polished Appearance

CHAPTER THREE

What Are Professional, Business Casual, and Uniform Attires?

*Y*our appearance tells people who you are and what you represent. Your outer appearance is critical to your professional success, no matter your age, profession, or position. When you care about the way you look, you build your confidence and project credibility. Your confidence will increase your chances for advancement and secure employment and reflect respect for yourself, your job, and your organization. Your appearance communicates your message before you even say a word.

When you do not care about your appearance, you diminish your chances for respect, credibility, and authority. Caring about your appearance isn't vain. When you do not care about yourself, you project low self-confidence, sloppiness, and lack of credibility. You do not have to wear the most expensive clothes or invest in cosmetic surgery, but you do need to appear smart, creative, and sharp.

The elements of your appearance include updated, age- and audience-appropriate clothing that fits and balances your body; styled hair; office-appropriate makeup; accessories; neat fingernails and toenails; and fresh personal hygiene. Your appearance should not be boring, outdated, or sloppy. You should make a good first impression. Here are three examples:

Example One

Susan is interviewing for a job for which she has all the necessary experience. In the waiting room at the interview, she sees two other applicants, a man and a woman. The man is wearing a navy suit with a white stayed shirt and a sharp tie. The woman is wearing a suit and looks polished from head to toe. Susan, on the other hand, is wearing wrinkled cotton pants, a casual printed shirt, and loafers. Does Susan get the job?

Even though we don't know the work experience of the other applicants or how they behaved in their interviews, we do know that first impressions are very important. Susan's interview attire was casual and sloppy. Her clothing suggested that her work would be sloppy, too. She lost her credibility.

Example Two

Nancy has just started her job as a high school principal. She wears Capri pants, short-sleeved tops, and sandals to work. After a few weeks on the job, she notices that her employees often ignore her policies. Why aren't Nancy's employees following her directions?

Principals are leaders of their schools. Nancy's work attire does not reflect her status. Her clothing does not differentiate her from her staff; students may not even identify her as the principal. Nancy's attire should state authority.

Example Three

Dawn is the assistant to the senior vice president at a large technology company. She comes in contact with clients, employees, and colleagues every day and does her job well. She usually wears pants, low-cut tops, and heavy makeup to work. Her boss has warned her to dress more conservatively, but she hasn't listened. Now she is up for a promotion.

Will Dawn be promoted? Probably not. Her attire is a little too risqué for work. Dawn should reexamine the company's dress code, adhere to it, and then try for the promotion again.

The three above examples demonstrate the importance of appropriate office attire. Even if you work from home or are a traveling businesswoman, your attire is important. Your appearance reflects on you not only when you're at work but when you're on vacation, out for the evening, or running errands. It is not unusual to strike up a conversation with someone outside of the office and have the conversation turn to work. You may be asked what you do. If you look unkempt or dated, you could lose a job offer or new client or customer and negatively affect your company's image. Just because you're off the clock doesn't mean you're off the radar—you never know whom you're going to meet!

Business attire can be confusing if . . .

- You don't know what is appropriate for your profession.
- You aren't familiar with your company's dress code policy.

There are three types of women's business attire: classic professional, business casual, and uniform. Here is detailed information on each type of dress.

PROFESSIONAL DRESS

The core of professional dress is a business suit: a jacket with matching skirt or pants. The suit should be lined and should fit well. With a suit, wear a blouse or camisole, appropriate jewelry, pantyhose, and close-toed, heeled shoes. Hair is styled, makeup is appropriate for the office, and face and nails are clean.

Professional dress has evolved a bit over time. In the 1700s and 1800s, men wore conservative business suits, in black, gray, navy, or pinstripe. In the twentieth century, there was a little more leniency and women began to enter the workforce in greater numbers. Suits for women replicated the cuts of suits for men, with skirts instead of pants. In the 1960s, pantsuits for women were introduced. As the twentieth century continued, women found suits with more angular cuts, new colors, and varied designs, along with more creative blouses, jewelry, and shoe styles.

Today, professional dress is still changing. Fabrics and blends are evolving, suit cuts accommodate different body shapes, and blouses may have vibrant patterns.

Professional Dress usually applies to:

- Interviewees and interviewers
- Lawyers and other people in court

- Television professionals
- Public speakers
- Consultants
- People in finance
- People in public relations
- Meeting planners
- Federal, state, city, and county officials
- Law enforcement professionals (excluding those who wear uniforms)
- People who work at the executive or management level
- Marketing and sales professionals
- Real estate professionals
- Staffing professionals
- Politicians
- Engineers
- Accountants
- Anyone who needs to project a refined, credible image.

Even if you do not work in one of the above professions, you should own a suit. You never know when you may need one.

A Classic Professional Dress Wardrobe

Suits: I suggest owning at least two. One should be red, black, navy, charcoal, or pinstripe; the other can be more creative. Don't be afraid to wear suits in pastels or vivid colors.

Blouses and Camisoles: Blouses and camisoles should be made of fabrics that complement your suits. Do not wear cotton tops with suits. (More on clothing elements in Chapter Six.)

Accessories: Accessories include earrings, necklaces, bracelets, pins, belts, scarves, watches, and glasses. These pieces are integral parts of your clothing message. I recommend wearing accessories, because they make your look POP! Make sure not to wear too many accessories, though—they should enhance your clothing, not distract from it.

Shoes: A variety of close-toed shoes look fabulous with suits. Consider pumps, sling-backs, square-toed shoes, and T-strap shoes. Your shoes should complement your suit.

Hose: While hose can be uncomfortable and hot for women, especially in the southern regions, they cultivate the classic professional dress image. Hose provide clean lines underneath garments, slenderize the body, and smooth out the legs.

Hair, Face, Nails, and Personal Hygiene: Hair should be styled; makeup should enhance, not overpower, your face; and nails should be groomed.

The second type of office attire is business casual. It is more versatile and comfortable than professional dress.

BUSINESS CASUAL ATTIRE

Business casual attire became more popular in the early 1990s. It was introduced to help alleviate employees' clothing expenses and increase morale. At first, there were casual Fridays, when employees were allowed to wear jeans and casual shirts. Casual Fridays were very popular, and soon some companies allowed more casual dress two or three days per week. Human resources professionals loosened their dress code policies. Some industries even noticed more creativity in their employees once they were allowed to dress more comfortably.

However, there were some problems. Some employees took advantage of business casual dress and started dressing sloppily or skimpily. Toward the end of the 1990s, some offices banned business casual dress.

I am going to show you how dressing in business casual attire can project character, credibility, and confidence. Business casual is harder to figure out than classic professional attire, but I am here to help you understand the different levels of this type of dress and which types of clothing make up each.

First, every profession is different in what it deems appropriate business casual. Some professions are more conservative; others are creative, relaxed, stylish, or edgy. But all professions want their employees to look sharp, smart, and clean. Wherever you work, check to see if your office has a dress code policy. See Box 3.

Box 3
Dress Code

All companies should have dress code policies. A dress code policy is a guide that allows employees to know and understand the accepted attire in that workplace. Some dress code policies are detailed; others are more lenient. If you are a human resources professional and your company does not have a dress code, you should develop one. If you own a small or home-based business, you also need to have a dress code.

When you start a job, the personnel department should give you its policy. Look it over and see what is expected; if you have questions, ask. If the company does not have a dress code policy, ask what is expected.

If you are a home-based business owner, you need to have a dress code policy for yourself and anyone who works for you. No matter what environment you are in, your reputation demands a sharp outer image.

Types of Business Casual

There are two types of business casual attire: smart and artistic. Smart is applicable to most professions, but artistic is appropriate for specialty professions.

Smart Business Casual

Smart business casual does not include denim, flip-flops, ripped or tattered clothing, multiple piercings, or visible tattoos. (If your profession allows any or all of the above, see artistic business casual.) As with any attire, smart business casual should fit your body frame, complement your skin and hair, project an updated style, and be age-appropriate. You will learn how to develop your style in the next few chapters.

Blazer: A blazer is the most classic element of business casual. It is always a good idea to have a blazer around. Even if you don't wear it all day, keep it nearby so that you can throw it on for a meeting or unexpected clients.

Blouses and Tops: Avoid sleeveless tops without blazers and all low-cut tops. Sleeves should be cap- to full-length. Choose tops that coordinate with your pants and skirts. (See more on creating outfits in Chapter Seven.)

Sweaters: Sweaters are great additions to a business casual wardrobe. Avoid sweaters that are too bulky. Consider knit sets, vests, and cardigans.

Slacks: Slacks made entirely of cotton tend to look sloppy. Your slacks should include polyester, microfiber, or Teflon blends in a variety of colors and weaves. Pants should be full-length, with a $1/2$-inch break in front and a hemline that stops $1/4$-inch from the shoe. They should not have pleated fronts. Capri and cropped pants are generally not appropriate for the workplace. If you are allowed to wear them, see artistic business casual. (See more in Chapter Six.)

Skirts: Skirts are staples of a business wardrobe. Wear skirts in lengths between three inches above the knee and mid-calf. Long skirts may be hazardous in the workplace because they can get caught on things.

Dresses: Dresses should be in structured shapes, with appropriate hemlines. Make sure your dresses do not date you.

Shoes: Depending on your company's dress code, everything from open-toed shoes to boots may be acceptable.

Accessories: Accessories complete your outfit. A wide variety of accessories may be acceptable.

Hair, Face, and Nails: Your hair may be styled or relaxed. Makeup should be appropriate for the office. Your fingernails and toenails should be groomed. (Grooming details are important. See more about them in Chapter Seven.)

Artistic Business Casual

In more creative industry professions such as fashion, entertainment, technology, gaming arts, photography, and interior design, you may see this type of attire. However, even with artistic dress, it is best to know your audience and what you want to communicate.

If your profession allows and encourages artistic dress, many different types of clothing may be allowed, including jeans, shorts, T-shirts, and sneakers. However, sloppy, dirty, or messy attire is not appropriate.

The third type of business attire is uniform attire. If you work in medicine, transportation, or manufacturing or at a theme park, supermarket, or hotel, you may be required to wear a uniform.

Uniform Attire

Uniform attire has been around as long as classic professional dress. Even if you wear a uniform, you have an image to project. You may not need to concentrate on what to wear, but your attention should be directed to the details of your uniform.

Your uniforms should be clean and pressed and should fit well. They should not be worn, faded, or torn. Coordinate with permitted accessories, and groom your hair and nails. Wear a nametag if that's required. Replace uniforms when necessary.

You have now learned why professional dress, smart business casual, artistic business casual, and uniform attire are important and what makes up each. In the following chapters, you will learn to positively influence an audience of one or many; create a wardrobe that reflects your own style, is age-appropriate, and fits and balances your body shape; and build an outfit option wardrobe. Your appearance plays a huge part in your professional success!

The next chapter is Calendar Dress. Calendar Dress will show you how to preplan your wardrobe, making it easy to prepare for each day.

CHAPTER FOUR

Calendar Dress

*I*n the last chapter I spoke briefly about the ways in which your dress attire communicates your message to an audience. In this chapter I am going to show you how to use what you wear to influence your audience. You start this by understanding calendar dress. Calendar dress is planning your wardrobe in advance to communicate your message to an audience of one or many.

What does it mean to communicate with your audience before you open your mouth?

You want your audience to see these character-istics in you:

- Authority
- Expertise
- Interest
- Credibility
- Confidence
- Character
- Leadership
- Education
- Experience
- Originality
- Honesty
- Responsibility

You first communicate your message with your appearance and follow it up with speaking intelligently and behaving with pride. (In Chapter Nine, I will teach you how to speak intelligently and in Chapter Eleven, I will teach you how to behave with pride.)

Element Two: A Polished Appearance

I want you to pull out your PDA or open your desk calendar. Look at all of your day's appointments; include functions before and after work. Remember that any schedule may change unexpectedly. After you look at a day, look at your week and month. For some appointments, you'll know exactly who your audience is going to be; at others, you'll be meeting new people.

Your calendar is a perfect way for you to determine what to wear. Often, women spend too much time in the morning standing in front of their closets trying to decide what to wear. My advice is to take a moment or two to create an outfit that will reflect your credibility, reputation, and authority. Your decision does not need to be a time-consuming one, but it should involve genuine thought. You should be able to pick an outfit that you feel confident wearing and spend more time preparing yourself mentally for your day.

In my line of work, I speak to many companies, organizations, schools, and individuals.

Whether my audience has one or one thousand members, it is important to me. The way I dress needs to communicate my expertise, my knowledge of the audience, and the message I want to communicate. I cater my dress to each of my audiences. For instance, if I am speaking to a group of female executives, I wear a suit, but if I am speaking to a moms' group, I wear slacks, a top, and a blazer. I dress differently because my audiences are different. You should show your audience that you understand it and are knowledgeable about it. When you dress without having your audience in mind, you come across as unprepared and incapable.

Understanding and applying calendar dress to your professional life is essential for your professional success. For instance, if you are a receptionist, your audience is everyone who enters the door during work hours, as well as those you might meet after hours. If you are a teacher, your audience consists of students, co-workers, administrators, parents, grandparents, and any other person with whom you come into contact. If you are a CEO, your audience consists of your employees, colleagues, clients, potential clients, company donors, and constituents. If you work in medicine, your audience consists of patients, other medical personnel, and patients' family and friends. Think of your position and how many people could be in your audience for the day, and don't forget surprise meetings and after-work events. Below, list your audiences:

_____

_____

_____

_____

_____

_____

_____

_____

_____

_____

Now that you are thinking about your calendar and your audiences, here are a few examples of how your appearance can affect your various audiences.

Example One: Your Audience Is Clients

Your calendar shows that you have no appointments today, so you wear jeans to work. However, at 4:00 P.M., a client unexpectedly stops by. What does your dress communicate?

Your extremely casual dress is not the way you normally dress. You usually wear professional or smart business casual. You meet with the client and tell him that you're wearing jeans because it's casual day and apologize for your attire. This could take care of the situation, but the client may be taken aback by your attire, which could lead to a decrease in his business.

Correction: If you are allowed to wear jeans on prescribed days, that's fine. Otherwise, wear smart business casual. It is also a good idea to have a blazer handy.

Example Two: Your Audience Is Clients

You work from home and come into contact with clients occasionally. One day, you receive a call from a client who wants to see you. You are wearing shorts and don't change before the meeting. When you arrive, the client greets you coldly and seems surprised. Why?

Your attire is way too casual. Your client trusts you to take care of her. Your attire does not signify credibility. Just because you work from home does not mean you can dress casually all the time.

Correction: Women who work from home need to design a credible dress code policy for themselves. I recommend smart business casual. You never know when you are going to meet a client. Be prepared!

Example Three: Industry Advancement

You work in the medical industry, wear a uniform, and have been told on two occasions to make sure that your uniform is pressed. You are up for a promotion, but you do not receive it, even though you had the same qualifications as the candidate who got the job. Why didn't you get the promotion?

You were reprimanded twice for your messy appearance. Because you reflect that you do not care about your current job, your employer feels that you would lack responsibility in a managerial role. Even though you have the necessary experience, your unprofessional image loses you the promotion. The company wants employees who have sharp images to represent them. Be careful—you could lose your current job.

Correction: Sharpen your uniform attire and show responsibility, then reapply for the management position.

Example Four: Industry Advancement

You are an expert in your field and your company relies on your expertise. You wear cargo pants and tank-tops to work every day. A better job opens at the company and you apply, knowing you have the necessary expertise. However, you don't get the job. Later, you hear that your appearance was a big factor.

Companies look for employees who are educated, have expertise, are experienced, possess leadership skills, and are team players, but they also look for sharp appearances. Cargo pants and tank-tops reflect college days.

Correction: Beat the competition and always look great, because that communicates respect for yourself and company and you never know who is looking at you. You need to wear professional dress, smart business casual or artistic business casual.

Example Five: Potential Clients

You are going to a morning chamber event. You are excited because there should be many potential clients in attendance. You decide to wear a casual skirt and polo shirt. When you arrive, you notice that some are in suits and other in sharp-looking business casual attire. You feel confident and mingle, but do not get any business cards or inquiries about your business. Why?

Element Two: A Polished Appearance

Your appearance is way too casual. Most chamber events require professional dress or smart business casual. You look too casual and this will hurt your business.

Correction: Whenever you have a chamber or networking event, you need to wear either a business suit or smart business casual attire with a blazer. If your event is in the evening, social business casual is appropriate. See transitional dress below.

Example Six: An Employee Audience

You are a vice president of human resources and govern fifteen hundred employees. Your company's dress code calls for smart business casual. In a normal week, you wear jeans, polo shirts, and sneakers. You hear from your department heads that the dress code is being ignored. You send an e-mail to everyone

> enforcing the dress code, but you contin-
> ue to dress very casually. Why aren't the
> employees responding?

You are in executive-level management and are not abiding by the dress code guidelines. Even though you are in management, you are not exempt from following the dress code. You must lead by example.

Correction: Your clothing should be a mix of smart business casual and classic professional dress.

Example Seven: Your Audience Is a Jury and Judge.

You are prepared for trial and have your research, exhibits, and dialogue organized and ready. You decide to wear a long dress and sandals. As you start presenting your case to the jury, you notice the jury and judge are bored. Why?

___

Your appearance is sloppy. Professional dress attire is not an option in court; it is mandatory. If you are an attorney, your appearance is a large part of your profession; it shows your authority, expertise, and credibility. When you dress sloppily or too casually, you lose respect and influence.

Correction: When you are in court, you should always wear a suit, hose, and close-toed shoes. Don't lose your credibility.

Example Eight: Entertainment Audience

You are a TV anchor and in the public eye. You get a lot of criticism about your appearance from viewers. Why?

___

If you are in the public eye, it is not uncommon to receive negative comments about your appearance, because everyone has their own opinion about how you should dress. However, to decrease the amount of criticism, your image should reflect your character and authority.

Correction: If you are an anchor, your clothing should be professional. Make sure your suit complements the backdrop of the set and your blouse complements your suit. If you are a reporter, wear either a suit or smart business casual—whatever fits with the story you are reporting and fits with the company's dress code policy.

Example Nine:
Audience Is a Potential
New Employer

It is a Saturday and you are running errands. You throw on an old T-shirt and ripped jeans. When you are inside a store,

you strike up a conversation while standing in line and realize you are speaking
with a recruiter for a company you would
like to work for. Will your appearance hurt
your job prospects?

This example shows that your after-hours appearance is important. With this example, the
four types of attire that I described do not apply. Transitional dress now applies, and I will
talk about it next. This example shows that you
should care about your appearance even on
weekends or when you're not at the office.

Correction: Even when you wear shorts or
social evening attire, your appearance should reflect your character, confidence, and credibility,
because you never know whom you will meet.

TRANSITIONAL DRESS

There are many reasons to adjust your wardrobe for different audiences. However, what if

you are interacting with people at night, over dinner, at a party, or somewhere outside of work? Smart business casual, classical business professional, or creative business casual attire may not be appropriate. The appropriate type of dress is transitional dress. Transitional dress allows you to go from one audience to another in a social atmosphere.

Blazer on hand: A blazer is a key clothing piece that adds credibility quickly. The blazer should be black, navy, taupe, brown, or tweed. These basic colors will coordinate with many outfits, and the blend will complement many types of fabric. Your blazer should be of good quality. (In Chapter Seven, I will talk more about investment shopping.) A blazer makes a casual outfit look dressier quickly.

Refresher Kit: A basic daytime refresher kit should include lipstick or lip gloss, powder, breath mints, hand cleanser or lotion, clear nail polish, a safety pin, and a nail file. If you get a run in your hose or break a nail, you can fix those problems quickly.

Evening Kit: An evening kit should not go in your purse, but can go in your attaché or briefcase. If you know you have an evening event or think you may be attending one, pack an evening kit. In it, include facial cleanser, a toothbrush and toothpaste or breath mints, a hair brush, a hair dryer (if you use one), hair accessories and hairspray, perfume, and appropriate evening jewelry.

Evening work socials dictate professionalism. You can refresh or redo your makeup (apply a little more for evening than for daytime), restyle your hair, freshen your breath, and reapply your perfume. This process will help you feel incredible for your evening event.

You may want to bring a social top or blouse that coordinates with the skirt or pants you wore to work for an evening event. You could also bring open-toed shoes, jazzy jewelry, or a fun belt.

So what have you learned from this chapter?

1 You face different audiences every day.

2 Your audience can have one or many members.

3 You need to display authority, expertise, interest, credibility, confidence, character, experience, honesty, responsibility, accountability, and dedication.

4 You should mold your attire to each audience during the day.

5 You can transition your outfit for events after work.

6 Your appearance represents you inside and outside of work.

Now it is time to create a style that projects originality but still portrays your reputation, credibility and authority.

CHAPTER FIVE

Develop Your Work Style

*H*ow do you reflect your character, credibility, and confidence in your wardrobe for your professional life? You need an Outfit Option™ Work Style (OOWS). Your OOWS projects your originality, credibility, authority, and reputation.

It takes patience and care to become proficient at OOWS. When you start reading this section, do not become overwhelmed. You will need to put the book down and brainstorm. Your work wardrobe should be practical, functional, sophisticated and stylish, age-appropriate, original, and crisp. It should also be:

- Practical, because everyone's budget is different
- Functional, because job duties can range from light to industrial
- Sophisticated, a style that will need to be updated occasionally
- Age-appropriate
- Appropriate for your body frame

In the process of creating an OOWS, you must be conscientious. Looking good is not about being the most slender or beautiful woman in the room; it's about loving who you are. Crafting a look for yourself is not vanity, but an empowerment that makes you feel good. Let's get started!

Design Your Style

Some women have a knack for dressing well. Others do not. A few think they dress well, but actually don't. However, you do not need to be a fashion expert to create an original look. All you need is a little creativity.

When you begin to create your style, you should first think about what is age-appropriate. See Box 4.

Box 4
Age-Appropriate
Workplace Clothing

Women often believe they do not have a problem with age-appropriate attire when, in fact, they do. Human resources professionals often ask me what to do when female employees wear low-cut tops, short hemlines, or clothing that is too tight, sloppy, or outdated. They ask me how to approach these women. I always tell them that their female employees may know that they are dressing inappropriately, but they also may not know.

Dressing appropriately does not mean dressing frumpily. You can look good in appropriate office attire.

Women should follow these guidelines when they dress for work:

- Necklines should not reveal cleavage when you are standing or leaning over. Wear a camisole if the neckline of your blouse is lowcut.
- Hemlines should extend past your rear end! Do not wear skirts that hit higher than three inches above your knee.
- Wear outfits that let you breathe. Tight clothing can make you look bulgy.
- Do not wear clothing with visible spaghetti straps.
- Give away or throw away dated clothing; makeup and hair should also look modern.
- Shoes should be appropriate for the office.

> If a woman wants to protect her good reputation, she must be responsible for the clothes she wears.

Besides choosing age-appropriate clothing, you also need research, understanding, development, and application to create your OOWS.

Research

When you are ready to develop your new style, you need to research styles that look good on your body frame. Research styles by reading about them, looking at different options in stores, and consulting friends and family.

Some outfits in fashion magazines are outlandish or pricey, but others can inspire you. When you visit clothing stores, look at what the mannequins are wearing. Visit fabric stores and view their handmade clothes. Some television personalities have great style and will give you ideas. Be observant of the clothing around you.

UNDERSTANDING

While I want you to look for styles everywhere, understand what is best for you, your body shape, and your budget. As with any new venture, this takes practice. Take small steps and you will not become frustrated.

DEVELOPMENT

After you have sorted out some of your ideas about your style, you need to develop the practicality of dressing that way. This could mean learning to coordinate outfits, buying the correct size to fit your body shape, adding accessories, or getting a new hairstyle. Don't take on too much at one time, or you will become frustrated and confused. Have your family and friends encourage you and give you constructive criticism.

APPLICATION

Your mirror can be your best friend. At the beginning of this book I asked you what your mirror reflects. Use it to look at your new Outfit Options, hair, and accessories. Sometimes a hairstyle is a small enough change to begin your transformation or renewal. Apply what you learned in your research, understanding, and development to your new work style image. Make the application a routine, and before you know it you will have created your unique style.

Here are some ideas for basic styles that you can build upon to create your own. You don't need to pigeonhole yourself into only one style; that will become boring and pricey. Mix styles up a little.

CLASSIC STYLE:
REFINED SIMPLICITY

You are probably familiar with this style. It is a staple of women's fashion. Some women wear clothing in a classic style almost exclusively, while others use it as a jumping-off point,

The Key Components
of Classic Dress

- Neutral colors
- Ornate but classy patterns
- Basic cuts
- Modest accessories
- Simply styled hair
- Natural makeup

DRAMATIC STYLE:
DYNAMICALLY BOLD

Some women look striking in dramatic attire; others are too timid to wear it. Dramatic style can be a difficult attire to wear because of the daring component, but women can possess some of it in their work and social wardrobes no matter how old they are.

Key Components
of Dramatic Style

- Vivid colors
- Creative patterns
- Defined cuts
- Sassy accessories
- Lustrous hair
- Rich, non-overpowering makeup

SPORTY/NATURAL STYLE:
SPUNKY ADVENTURER

This style has a freedom about it. It is comfortable but spirited. You will see sporty styles in more relaxed areas of the country. This style is casual and carefree with a bit of edge. This style is not as prominent as other basic styles worn at work because sometimes it is too casual.

Key Components of Sporty/Natural Style

- Neutral or brushed colors
- Solids; few patterns
- Relaxed cuts
- Basic accessories, if any
- Traditional hair
- Little or no makeup

TRENDY STYLE: SASSY VERSATILITY

The trendy style reflects the latest fashions. This style may include some pieces that are not wardrobe staples and become dated quickly; however, this style projects modern edginess. Make sure to wear only what is appropriate for your age, though. Not all workplaces allow trendy clothing, but many do.

Key Components
of Trendy Style

- Versatile colored palette schemes
- Eclectic cuts
- Artistic designs and patterns
- Unique and flashy accessories
- Modern hairstyles
- The latest makeup

POETIC STYLE:
FRESH AND FEMININE

Poetic style includes romantic, soft, or "nostalgic" clothing, like peasant blouses. It has changed drastically over the decades and is continually being updated to stay current.

Key Components
of Poetic Style

- Soft colors
- Floral designs
- Ruffled and lace embellishments
- Flouncy cuts
- Demure hair
- Fresh makeup

Now that you have finished your style discovery homework and have seen the characteristics of the various styles, it is time for you to determine. your combined style.

COMBINED STYLE

A combined style allows you diversity in each Outfit Option and saves money. If you were to pick only one style and wear it routinely, you would get bored and become a routine dresser again. A combined style means choosing two, three, four, or all five basic styles and melding them into one. (You can use this process for your casual and social styles, too). By now, you should have a good idea of the styles that interest you. Some may be familiar ones you already wear, but I hope you found some that you want to try. Get out of your comfort zone and try a classic, dramatic, sporty, poetic, or trendy piece. Remember to take small steps.

I recommend using my percentage system to develop your unique combination of styles. For instance, one day you want your outfit to look eighty percent classic and twenty percent dramatic. Another day, you want your outfit to be sixty percent trendy, twenty percent classic, and twenty percent poetic. The total should always reach one hundred percent. The key to a correct style combination is knowing your audience. For instance, let's say you are meeting with a potential employer. I would recommend a more classic style with a bit of the dramatic. If you are in an artistic profession and leading a meeting with colleagues, I recommend mixing trendy, classic, and poetic styles. If you are an executive in a classic professional dress atmosphere and are meeting clients, wear classic with dashes of dramatic and trendy styles. If you own a home-based business, you can wear elements of all five styles.

In this chapter, you learned how to create your Outfit Option™ Work Style. Now you are ready to discover how clothes can complement your body shape and give you a sleek silhouette. Chapter Six shows you how!

Accentuate Your Body Frame

*O*ne of the biggest challenges for women, no matter how old they are, is choosing the clothes that look best on their body frame and give them a comfortable sense of style. My company conducted a clothing survey of two hundred men and women of different ages in 2006. Women said that their biggest challenge was finding clothing that fit properly, and their second biggest challenge was finding clothing that was appropriate but stylish for the thirty-and-above age group. To find clothes that look good and fit you properly, you must understand your body frame and learn which clothing elements accentuate it.

All women have body assets! You may think you do not have any, but you do. As I mentioned before, you do not need to be the most beautiful or have the best body. While I want you to be healthy and in shape, I am going to teach you how to wear clothing that accentuates your body shape.

We will talk more about challenging areas later in this chapter, but for now I want you to focus on your body assets. Do you have beautiful eyes, a welcoming smile, great skin, healthy hair, a nice bust, a slim waist, a proportioned body shape, toned legs, etc.? List your body assets here:

_____

_____

_____

_____

_____

Did that take you a long time? I hope not. You are not being vain; rather, you are taking the first step toward accentuating your body frame while pumping up your self-esteem.

Your body is three-dimensional, with a front view, a back view, and a side view. When you get dressed for the day, you should pay attention to all three views. When you are in front of an audience, even though they should focus on your face, they will look at your whole body. So pay attention to all views.

DISCOVER YOUR BODY FRAME

It is time for you to look at your body frame. Remember, do not start off by criticizing your body because you will get too frustrated and defeat the purpose. You need to learn about your body frame so that you can project a balanced silhouette.

Almost every woman's basic body shape is an "hourglass":

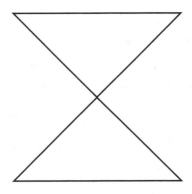

If you were to have somebody trace your body onto a piece of paper, this is probably what you would see. No matter whether you are heavy, thin, short, or tall, your basic body shape from the front view is probably an "hourglass." Don't you wish I could stop right there? Unfortunately, I can't, because as well as front views, we all have side and back views! When you get dressed for the day, you must consider all three views. You must learn about your body shape so that you can create a flattering silhouette.

Here's how to discover your shape beyond the "hourglass."

Element Two: A Polished Appearance

You will need

- A full-length mirror
- A handheld mirror
- Good lighting
- Enough room to turn around and extend your arms
- Fitted casual top and bottom (T-shirt and gym shorts or yoga pants)
- Measuring tape
- A piece of paper and writing utensil (optional)

First, determine your front view body frame. Besides the "hourglass," you have another front view.

1 Look in your mirror at your shoulders, waist, and hips.
2 Are your shoulders wider than your hips or vice versa?
3 Does your waistline dip inward?
4 Do you carry your weight in your torso, waist, hips, or thighs?

If you have never focused on your body frame, it may take you a few minutes to answer these questions. Ask a family member to give you his or her opinion.

Inverted Triangle

Your shoulders are wider than your hips.

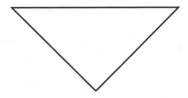

Triangle

Your hips are wider than your shoulders.

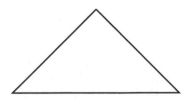

Rectangle

Your waistline does not dip inward.

Pear

You carry more weight in your hips and thighs than on top.

You have identified your secondary front view body frame. Now you need to identify your side and back views and determine your body features. Since you already know your body assets, you now need to find your challengeing areas.

Look at your body again. This time, take a more detailed look at your front, back, and side views and fill in the chart on the next page. If it is a body asset, mark it as an asset; if it is a challenging area, mark it as a challenge. Also fill in your measurements.

Well done! You have now discovered your overall body shape; you know your front, back, and side views; you know your assets and challenging areas. You also know your measurements; this will help if you ever want clothes made for you.

The goal of accentuating and balancing your body frame requires learning the elements of clothing and knowing which pieces look good on you. When you understand the elements, it will be much easier for you to buy clothes that make you look fantastic and balance your body frame. Let's look at the elements of clothing.

Element Two: A Polished Appearance

Body Feature	Asset	Challenge	Oval	Round	Diamond	Heart	Pear	Oblong	Measure
Face									
Eyes									
Smile									
Hair									
Neck			Normal	Short	Long	Full	Skinny		
Shoulders			Normal	Sloping	Narrow	Broad	Uneven		
Arms			Normal	Full Upper Arm	Fleshy Upper Arm	Thick Elbows			
Bust			Average Fullness	Small	Full	High Lift	Low Lift	Average Lift	
Torso			Balanced	Short-Waisted	Long-Waisted				
Tummy			Flat	Average	Full				
Waist			Defined						
Hips			Normal	Slim	Narrow	Wide	Even	Uneven	
Derriere			Normal	Flat	Low	High	Small	Full	
Thighs			Normal	Small	Average	Full	Defined	Loose	
Knees			Normal	Skinny	Full		Defined		
Calves			Normal	Small	Full	Defined	Loose		

93

ELEMENTS OF CLOTHING

The four elements of clothing are cut, fabric, pattern, and color. It is important to know and understand these elements, because the more you learn about how to craft an outfit to balance your body frame, the better you will look. Don't worry, you do not need to be a fashion designer. But you do need to open your mind to a variety of cuts, fabrics, patterns and designs, and rich colors.

Cut

"Cut" is what you may know as "fit." Clothing designers cannot make clothes to fit every body frame, but some are better at it than others. You need to buy clothes that fit your body frame and are not too small or too big. This is a good time to reiterate the importance of age-appropriate clothing, as discussed in Chapter Five.

Try on clothes to make sure they fit your frame. You do not want your clothes to stretch too tightly across your bust, reveal fat rolls, or pull across your hips. Clothing should fit you well whether you are standing, walking, squatting, or reaching. Below are some universal cut tips that accentuate and balance your body frame:

Blouses/Tops

- Buy tops with a princess cut:

- A princess-cut top has seams that start near the underarm and cascade inward toward the top's bottom hem. These seams are hidden in blouses and visible in T-shirts. Pay attention if you have a rectangular body shape—princess tops can define your waist. They're great for all body shapes.

- Buy tops that sit on your shoulder but fall no more than $1/4$-inch down the shoulder.
- Buy tops that grace your torso. They should not be too tight.

Suit Jackets

- Buy suit jackets and blazers whose lapels lay flat and are not wrinkled.
- Your arms should fit well through the jacket's armholes. Sleeve length should hit at mid-thumb.
- The jacket should be fully lined.
- Buttons that match the jacket color are the most professional.

Pants

- First concentrate on whether your pants fit your hips. The side seams and side pockets should not pull. Pants that fit your hips may not fit your waist, but don't worry if they don't—waists can be taken in, but side seams usually can't be let out. Try on pants with shoes.

- In general, do not buy pants with pleats; they add weight to your mid-section. If you are tall and slender, you may be able to wear pleats.
- The hemline should not be too short.

Skirts and Dresses

- Skirts and dresses should not be too short. They should hit three inches above your knee or below.
- Make sure the skirt's seams do not pull across your hips.
- Most women look the best in A-line skirts.

An important note: when you try on clothes, find your size but do not dwell on it. The cut or fit is what needs your attention. See Box 5.

Box 5
Sizing

You wear a size 10 in slacks and you are in the market for a black pair. At the clothing store you try on a size 10 but they are too tight. You don't think you have gained weight and are surprised the size does not fit. Stop right there! You may have gained weight, but before jumping to that conclusion, there are other reasons the slacks may not fit you. Often, even if clothing comes from the same manufacturer, sizes are not exact. You may try on one size 10 and it is too tight; try another and it will probably fit. Also, sometimes clothing store sales personnel mismark clothing, or the clothing manufacturer may put the wrong size on the label.

FABRIC

Fabric is an integral part of the goal of a balanced body. Have you ever looked at labels to see what kinds of fabric you are buying? Probably not. Fabric types determine whether clothes look good and are comfortable, durable, and sophisticated. You need to understand the different types of fabric.

Fabric is made of fibers. Some fabrics are made of natural fibers; others are synthetic. Some fabrics are woven, others blended. Some fabrics are more absorbent than others. Some fabrics wrinkle, and others are wrinkle resistant. Let's take a close look at fabric details.

- **Natural fibers** like wool, silk, and linen are absorbent, decrease static electricity, and are of high quality and excellent longevity. They also wrinkle more and are expensive. Good for suits, shirts, and slacks.

- **Synthetic fibers** like polyester, spandex, rayon, Teflon, and acrylic wrinkle less, hold their shape better, provide more comfort, and cost less. They can have more static electricity and are sometimes less absorbent. Good for slacks, shirts, and some suits.

Fabrics made of natural and synthetic fibers are excellent for work clothing. Buy slacks made of wool or polyester fabrics; they look sharp, drape nicely, and provide comfort. Stayed and button-down collared shirts made of pima or merino cotton are quality shirts. Look for these fabrics not only in your long-sleeved shirts, but also in your short-sleeved and polo shirts.

- **Blended fabrics** are a mix of natural and synthetic fibers. Common mixes are poly/rayon and cotton/rayon/spandex. Blended fibers wrinkle less, provide comfort, and hold their shape.

They also can be expensive. They are good for some short-sleeved shirts and shorts.

- **Woven fabrics** include twill, jacquard, and houndstooth. They are strong, wrinkle resistant, warm, and sharp-looking. However, they can be expensive and snag easily. They are good for blazers, suits, skirts, and slacks.

You should own a little bit of each category above. Otherwise, your work wardrobe may be expensive or inflexible. Also, certain fabrics are best for certain types of garments.

Fabrics should drape with structure; the shape of garments should not collapse. When fabrics do not accentuate body shapes or do not blend well, they add weight and make the outfit look cheap. A rule of thumb when you combine separates made of different fabrics is to make sure that there is a percentage of the same fabric in each piece.

Now that you have a greater understanding of fabric, look in your closet and see what you own. Your work wardrobe should include all of these fibers and fabrics. When you start to wear more polished fabrics, your credibility, authority, reputation, and confidence will increase, making you feel good and helping you to influence others.

PATTERNS

Clothing designers have provided women with a plethora of clothing in different patterns. Credibility and authority do not decrease when you mix a creative pattern with a solid, or when you wear a pinstriped suit with a solid shirt. Rather, the character you add to your outfit projects your confidence.

Feeling uncomfortable wearing patterns is not uncommon. My female clients and seminar attendees often tell me that they have never worn patterns or do not know how to wear them. I have influenced many of them to break out of their "comfort zones," and now they love patterns!

Start incorporating patterned clothing into your work wardrobe slowly. Try a blouse with simple vertical lines, a short-sleeved blouse with splashes of color, or a mosaic-print three-quarter-sleeve top. Wear it, see how you like it, and I am sure you will get compliments on it. Another benefit of patterned clothing in your work wardrobe is that it can disguise challenging areas and highlight body assets. For example, a dress with vertical stripes can make your body look slimmer.

Two things to consider when choosing patterns are scale and combination.

Scale

Scale is the balance of the patterns on the garment piece. You can have an individual pattern such as polka dots, vertical or horizontal lines, flowers, or plaids. Medium-scaled patterns look best on most body frames. For instance, if you have a full tummy, a solid may showcase it while a pattern will disguise it. Pay attention to your body features when choosing patterns. You do not want them to accentuate your challenging areas. Scale of patterns is important!

Combination

Combination is the mixing of different patterns together. It can be hard to combine patterns; a mixture usually looks best on tall, lean body shapes, because the scale of the mixed patterns helps give dimension. Trendy dressers also often like to combine styles. The key to mixing patterns is to use similar colors with the same fabric textures.

COLOR

Color is vivid and brilliant. It makes the wearer feel good and sends positive and powerful messages. Think about a time when you wore a colorful shirt. Did you look in the mirror and say, *"Wow, I look great!"*? Or did you receive a compliment on the way you dressed? Doesn't that feel good?! All women should wear color because it slims, highlights, and shows character. Can you tell I am a huge proponent of women wearing color? I want you to become one too! Many women feel uncomfortable wearing color for the same reasons they feel uncomfortable wearing patterns—they think color draws too much attention to them. However, color can accentuate your body and enliven your face. If you do not like wearing color, be open-minded and take small steps.

How do you know if a color is good for you? Take the mirror test. It will definitely help you know which colors look best on you.

Mirror Test

1   Wear clothing in a neutral color.

2   Stand in front of a mirror and make

sure there is good lighting.

3 Take one of your shirts and hold it up to your face while looking at the mirror.

4 If you see a healthy glow in your face, that shirt is a good color for you. If the color washes you out, it is not a good color for you. If you aren't sure, ask a family member.

I believe that you can wear almost any color if you adjust its hue or intensity to complement your skin color, hair, and eye color. If you like a color but it does not like you, change its hue or intensity to make it love you. Think of the pictures you take with your digital camera: you can adjust their hue or intensity to make them look crisper. That is exactly what you can do with color.

Colors can be slimming. Some slimming colors include:

■ Black

- Red
- Navy
- Chocolate brown
- Mulberry
- Olive
- Green
- Turquoise
- Raspberry

When you walk into the office, meet a client, present a seminar, or make a presentation, your clothing color talks. Color can represent authority, creativity, character, confidence, power, and influence. For instance, a black suit shows authority, and a red suit shows empowerment. A patterned business casual top with a solid-colored skirt shows creative confidence. Think of your audience when you dress for the day, because your color will communicate your credibility.

You now know your body frame, the elements of clothing, and the importance of each to project a balanced shape with a sophisticated style. In the next chapter, I am going to show you how to build and plan your Outfit Option™ Work Wardrobe. But first, I would like to give you recommendations for incorporating the elements of coloring with different body shapes to project a complementary silhouette.

RECOMMENDATIONS BASED ON YOUR BODY FRAME

Look at your Body Feature Chart and pay attention to my recommendations. I am going to outline cuts, fabrics, patterns, and colors that complement all body features. Also remember the age-appropriate guidelines when choosing outfits, buying them, and wearing them. Use these recommendations to create your overall accentuating silhouette.

Neck

IF YOUR NECK IS OF AVERAGE LENGTH

Most flattering

- Most collars—V-neck, crewneck, etc.

IF YOUR NECK IS SHORT

Most flattering

- V-necks
- U-shaped necks
- Long necklaces
- Medium-length hair

Avoid

- Turtlenecks
- Crewnecks
- Choker necklaces

IF YOUR NECK IS LONG

Most flattering

- Turtlenecks
- Crewnecks
- Shorter necklaces
- Tops with medium-sized patterns
- Medium-length hair

Avoid

- Exaggerated V-, U-, and square-necks
- Short haircuts
- Long necklaces

Shoulders

IF YOUR SHOULDERS ARE OF AVERAGE WIDTH

Most flattering

- Shirts whose seams hit at the shoulders or $1/4$-inch off them

IF YOUR SHOULDERS ARE SLOPING OR NARROW

Most flattering

- Natural-looking shoulder pads
- Shirts with set-in sleeves and structured shoulders
- Shirts with boatnecks
- Shirts with medium-sized patterns

Avoid

- Raglan, dropped, and dolman shoulders

Element Two: A Polished Appearance

IF YOUR SHOULDERS ARE BROAD

Most flattering

- Raglan, dropped, and dolman shoulders
- Mosaic prints
- Light-colored tops

Avoid

- Set-in shoulders
- Shoulder pads
- Boatneck collars

Arms

IF YOUR ARMS ARE OF AVERAGE THICKNESS

Most flattering

- Any sleeve length, from cap- to full-length sleeves

IF YOUR UPPER ARMS ARE FULL OR FLESHY

Most flattering

- Three-quarter- or full-length sleeves
- Gathered cap sleeves

Avoid
- Sleeveless shirts

IF YOUR FOREARMS ARE FULL OR FLESHY
Most flattering
- Three-quarter- or full-length sleeves
- Patterns

Avoid
- Sleeveless shirts

Bust

No matter what your bust size is, invest in supportive seamless bras. They support and elongate your torso. They are a must!

IF YOUR BUST IS OF AVERAGE FULLNESS
Most flattering
- A supportive seamless bra
- Draped fabric

- Flattering necklines

Avoid

- Low necklines
- Tight clothing

IF YOUR BUST IS SMALL

Most flattering

- A supportive seamless bra
- Medium-sized patterns, short necklaces, and earrings that drive the focus upward

Avoid

- Tight clothing
- Low necklines

IF YOUR BUST IS LARGE

Most flattering

- A supportive seamless bra
- Accessories that drive the focus upward

- Draping fabric

Avoid

- Tight clothing
- Low necklines
- Small patterns

Torso

IF YOUR TORSO IS SHORT

Most flattering

- Princess-cut tops and jackets
- Semi-fitted and untucked tops
- Bias-cut tops
- Tops with vertical stripes
- Empire tops
- Medium-sized patterns
- With pants that have belt loops, a
  $1^{1}/_{2}$ to 2-inch-wide, solid-colored belt

Avoid

- Tight tops
- Very short jackets

IF YOUR TORSO IS LONG

Most flattering

- Princess-cut tops, cut on the bias and tucked in
- 2- to 3-inch-wide belts
- Shorter jackets in a princess-cut and duster jackets

Avoid

- Pants with low waistbands
- Drop belts

Tummy

IF YOUR TUMMY IS FLAT

Most flattering

- Flat-fronted pants with no waistband or with belt loops

Avoid

- Pleated pants

IF YOUR TUMMY IS NOTICEABLE

Most flattering

- Flat-fronted pants
- Jackets with structured shoulders and peplum jackets
- Fabrics that drape nicely
- Princess-cut, semi-fitted tops
- Tops with medium-sized patterns, diagonal patterns, and gathered sides
- Tops whose hemlines hit right below the most prominent part of your stomach

Avoid

- Tight or tent-like clothing
- Breaks in color that hit at the most prominent part of your stomach
- Pleated pants

Waist

IF YOUR WAIST IS DEFINED

Most flattering

- Medium-sized patterns

Classic professional attire

Authoritative classic professional attire

Classic professional attire

Sporty, smart business casual attire

Trendy, artistic business casual attire

Classic business casual attire, good for social events

Proper uniform attire

Trendy business casual attire,
good for social events

Poetic business casual attire

Artistic, poetic business casual attire

Polyester fabrics, great for blouses, skirts, and jackets

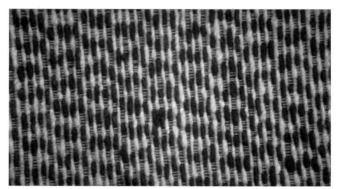

Woven fabric, great for blazers and suits

Patterned fabric, great for social blouses, slacks, and suits

- Princess-cut tops, suit jackets, and blazers
- Semi-fitted tops
- Flat-fronted pants

Avoid

- Rectangular side seams

IF YOUR WAIST IS UNDEFINED

Most flattering

- Medium-sized patterns
- Princess-cut and semi-fitted tops
- Diagonal patterns
- Gathered or shirred-side tops
- Flat-fronted pants

Avoid

- Rectangular side seams
- Boxy jackets and suits

Hips

IF YOUR HIPS ARE OF AVERAGE WIDTH

Most flattering

- Flat- or dart-fronted pants

- Pants with no front pockets or with hidden front pockets
- Pants with no back pockets or with slit or flip back pockets
- Pinstripes
- Skirts of almost any cut

Avoid

- Side pockets

IF YOUR HIPS ARE WIDE

Most flattering

- Flat- or dart-fronted pants
- Pants with no front pockets or with hidden front pockets
- Pants with no back pockets or with slit or flip back pockets
- Solid-colored pants
- A-line, inverted pleat, or cascade pleat skirts
- Jackets

Avoid

- Tight pants and skirts
- Light-colored pants and skirts if you are not wearing a jacket

Bottom

IF YOUR BOTTOM IS OF AVERAGE SIZE

Most flattering
- Follow the guidelines for women with average-sized hips

IF YOUR BOTTOM IS FLAT OR LOW

Most flattering
- Back pockets that sit high on your pants
- Draping fabric

Avoid
- Pants with no pockets or low pockets

IF YOUR BOTTOM IS HIGH

Most flattering
- Medium-placed pockets

Avoid
- High pockets

IF YOUR BOTTOM IS SMALL

Most flattering
- High back pockets
- Draping fabric, to add volume

Avoid
- Large pockets

IF YOUR BOTTOM IS FULL

Most flattering
- Flip pockets or pockets on only one side
- Draping fabric, to disguise fullness

Avoid
- Large pockets
- Tight pants

Thighs

IF YOUR THIGHS ARE OF AVERAGE SIZE

Most flattering
- Flat-fronted pants
- Draping fabrics
- Semi-fitted pants with straight or slightly flared legs
- Solids and pinstripes

Avoid
- Tight pants and skirts

Element Two: A Polished Appearance

Most flattering

- Semi-fitted, slightly flared pants
- Solids
- Skirts with a slight A-line

Avoid

- Tight pants
- Rectangular-cut legs
- Straight-legged pants
- Tight skirts

Knees

IF YOUR KNEES ARE OF AVERAGE SIZE

Most flattering

- Hemlines that hit between 3 inches above the knee and 3 inches below the knee

IF YOUR KNEES ARE FULL

Most flattering

- Skirts or dresses with hemlines that hit at the knee or 2 inches below it

Ankles

IF YOUR ANKLES ARE OF AVERAGE SIZE

Most flattering
- Pants that hit $1/2$- to 1 inch above the ground
- If you are allowed to wear Capri or cropped pants, they should hit 4 to 6 inches above the ankle, depending on your height

Avoid
- Pants that are too short

IF YOUR ANKLES ARE THICK

Most flattering
- Full-length pants with a slightly flared leg

Avoid
- Capri or cropped pants

Apply these recommendations to each of your body features and your overall appearance will be balanced, accentuating your silhouette!

CHAPTER SEVEN

Build and Plan Your Outfit Option™ Work Wardrobe

*n*ow that you have the practical tips to create a balanced silhouette, let's start creating an Outfit Option™ Work Wardrobe (OOWW). What is an Outfit Option™ Work Wardrobe? It is a practical, functional, stylish work wardrobe with at least two outfits for each work day or audience. The OOWW helps you build outfits, make good clothing investments, and pull your look together with good grooming, makeup, and hair. You will have more outfits for work and save money.

A woman's work schedule is busy, filled with decision-making, meetings, presentations, phone calls, and business travel. With so many tasks on your plate, you don't have much time to spend on deciding what to wear. The OOWW helps you make the right decisions about what to wear. Before we start the OOWW process, remember these questions:

- Does your outfit project your style?
- Does your outfit balance and accentuate your body frame?
- Is your outfit age-appropriate?
- Does the outfit adhere to your company's dress code?
- Does your appearance communicate your message?
- Does your outfit enhance your self-image?

Pick a weekend day to plan your OOWW. Depending on how large your wardrobe is, OOWW planning may take you two hours. If you find yourself becoming frustrated or impatient, take a break. When you have finished, you will feel accomplished!

BUILD YOUR WARDROBE

You have probably been trying to mix and match your clothes since you were a child. When you look polished, you may hear, *"Wow, you look great today!"* Doesn't that make you feel good? It is fun to be complimented. It is time to look great every day.

The work clothes in your closet are the best place to start building your wardrobe. When I am helping a client build her wardrobe, we start from her closet. This allows her to see if she currently owns clothes that would work in her new style, to mix and match those clothes to build new outfits, and to plan new additions to her wardrobe.

Before you start the building and planning process, you need to ready yourself. It is very important to style your hair and wear makeup as you would if you were going to work. This step helps you to see how your outfits will really look at the office.

Are you ready?

CLOSET REVISITED

By now, you should have decided on your personal style. Look in your closet and see if you have any pieces of clothing that fit with that style.

Get ready

1   Make sure your closet or room has good lighting.
2   Make sure you have enough room to move around.
3   Find an area near your closet where you can place clothes, like a bed.
4   Buy non-wire hangers.

5 Remember to consider work clothes that are in the laundry or at the cleaners!

Inspect Your Clothes

First, look at each piece of clothing in your closet to see if it is worn, spotted, faded, or damaged. You do not want to walk into your office with stained, outdated, worn, faded, or damaged clothes.

Next, separate your casual home clothes and evening social clothes from your work clothes. For now, I want you to focus only on your work wardrobe.

Now you can start sorting. Here's how it works, using pants as an example.

1 Select one pair of pants.
2 In good lighting, thoroughly examine those pants. Check the waistband, legs, knees, hemline, and back.

3 Check for wear, fading, holes, missing buttons, zipper problems, and torn hemlines.

4 If the pants have any of the problems listed above, put them in Pile 1.

5 If the pants are in great condition, try them on for fit and style. Do they accentuate your body frame? Do they reflect your new style?

6 If the answer to 5 is yes, put the slacks in Pile 2.

7 If the slacks are dated but accentuate your body frame, see if any alterations could be made and put them in Pile 3. See Box 6.

Box 6
Alterations

Alterations can often save a piece of clothing and make it look new. Let's say you own a dress that is well-made, but has a damaged bottom. Take the dress to the tailor and see if he or she can fix the dress's bottom or even turn it into a blouse. Or maybe you own a quality jacket that is from the 1980s and looks dated. Maybe a tailor could sew on more modern buttons, shorten the jacket, or remove its big shoulder pads to make it look current.

If a piece of clothing is too old, faded, or damaged, alterations won't work and you will end up wasting money. In that case, your best option is to invest in a new piece of clothing.

Now you should have three piles. Take a look at them—they are very important.

Pile 1 is the clothing you either need to give away or throw away. Donate clothing to a nonprofit organization if it's still wearable. If it's not, throw it away.

Pile 3 is the clothing that needs alterations before it can be included in your new look. Take it to the tailor's as soon as possible.

Pile 2 is the clothing for the foundation of your new look!

You have completed the first step of the building and planning process! You found clothes in your closet that fit you and define your new style. Now, let's move to the mix-and-match step.

MIX + MATCH = OUTFIT OPTIONS™!

Before you can start this step, you must have picked your clothes up from the tailor. You will also need:

1 Good lighting
2 A full-length mirror

3   A large handheld mirror

4   All your accessories (ties, shoes, and
        belts.)

5   Styled hair

6   Room to move around

7   A pen or pencil

8   Outfit Option™ Worksheet (OOW)

9   Time

Please look at number 8, OOW. You will find
a worksheet in the back of this book where
you can write down your outfit combinations
after you have created each one. By notating
your outfits, you will take the confusion out
of mixing and matching your clothing for the
audience of your day. The OOW is an excellent way to train yourself to coordinate outfits.
In time you will not even need it because you
will have the knack of Mix +Match = Outfit
Options™!

Let me remind you again to pay attention
to color, cut, fabric, pattern, style, and age-

appropriateness. Grooming details are also important. See Box 7.

Box 7
Grooming Details

What are grooming details? They are those little tweaks to your appearance you must pay attention to, because if you don't, it could cost you dearly in your professional success.

1. Look at your front, back, and side views.
2. Check for missing buttons, zipper problems, torn hemlines, etc.
3. Make sure your clothes are pressed.
4. Make sure your clothes are not too tight, outdated, or sloppy.
5. Make sure your shoes are intact and polished. Make sure their heels are not worn out.

---

6. Make sure that your hair and makeup are office-appropriate.

7. Make sure that you smell good, but that your perfume, if you wear it, is not overpowering.

It only takes a minute to look at yourself and do a once-through to make sure you have all your details in check. It can save you from embarrassment, being reprimanded, losing a client, or losing a job. Take pride in your appearance!

LET'S MAKE SOME OUTFITS!

1   Start with a pair of pants.

2   Find a top that matches them.

3   Add accessories: a belt, earrings, etc.

4   Look at your front, back, and side views in the mirror.

5   Ask yourself if the outfit you have created projects your new style.

6   If the answer to number 5 is yes, determine the audience for whom the outfit is appropriate, then catalog it in a chart. An example chart is below.

Clothing Item	Combine with:	Accessories	Audience	Plan to buy ...
Black woolen pants	Red and black top; red and black top with black jacket	Silver neck-lace and earrings; black shoes or boots	Coworkers; for leading a meeting	
Mulberry flat-front pants	Cream-and-mulberry sweater set	Cranberry necklace and belt; earrings; brown shoes		

You have done an excellent job creating Outfit Options™. Take a moment to sit back and look at your accomplishment!

Now, let's evaluate your wardrobe.

EVALUATE YOUR WARDROBE

You have created your Outfit Option™ Work Wardrobe and even a shopping list. Did you find new outfits during this process? You probably did. Did you use your accessories correctly? You probably did. Did you discover that some clothes you already owned could work with your new style? You probably did.

Did you discover you have some pieces that don't match anything else you own? You probably did. Did you discover you are in need of some additional clothes in a certain category? You probably did. Did you find that you need accessories? You probably did. All of this is part of evaluating your closet wardrobe: viewing what you have created and seeing what you need.

Write down what you need in your chart. Here is an example chart:

Clothing Item	Combine with:	Accessories	Audience	Plan to buy . . .
Black woolen pants	Red and black top; red and black top with black jacket	Silver necklace and earrings; black shoes or boots	Coworkers; for leading a meeting	
Mulberry flat-front pants	Cream-and-mulberry sweater set	Cranberry necklace and belt; earrings; brown shoes		
Purple bouclé suit	N/A	Pearl necklace	Meetings; presentations	Lavender or cream blouse
Gray suit with blue pinstripes	N/A	Long blue faux pearls and earrings	Meetings; after-hours social	Blue blouse

The suits above need blouses to go with them, and so the "Plan to buy . . ." column above suggests possible blouses to buy. Write down anything you need to buy in the "Plan to buy . . ." column.

Evaluating your closet helps you know what you have, what you need, and what you need more of. For example, if you only own one suit, but your company's dress code requires you to wear professional dress every day, you should buy two or three more suits so that you don't wear the same thing every day.

Accessories may be on your shopping list as well.

ACCESSORIES

As I said before, accessories make your outfit pop! Here are guidelines for a few types of accessories. Consider your profession, and determine what would work best for you.

Jewelry

Necklaces, earrings, pins, rings, and bracelets are staples. Invest in costume jewelry for work; you can afford more of it and coordinate it with all your outfits. Consider semi-precious, jewel-toned, braided, corded, and beaded jewelry. You may even be an expert at making your own. When you choose jewelry, make sure it coordinates with your outfit and isn't distracting.

Belts

Belts are stylish additions to an outfit. Navy, black, and tan belts are staples; consider fashionable belts as well. Belts can define your waist or distract from your tummy. Make sure your belt coordinates with your shoes.

Scarf

Scarves come in various sizes, lengths, and designs and can add a lot to your wardrobe. Depending on the scarf, you can wear it as a "necklace" or belt, or with a suit. You can find a book at your local bookstore about the various ways to tie a scarf.

Shoes

I love shoes! When you pick out shoes for work, make sure they are appropriate. For example, wear close-toed, heeled shoes with skirt suits. With pants, depending on your company's dress code policy and the season, you can wear heels, boots, mules, or open-toed heeled shoes. You do not need a separate pair of shoes for each outfit, but make sure to have at least a couple of pairs of shoes in neutral colors that can be worn with almost anything.

Purses

I recommend buying at least one well-made purse in a neutral color. The purse should not be too big or too small, and the color should work with any outfit and in any season.

Glasses

It is fun to wear whimsical glasses, but do not go over the top or date yourself. Wear frames in solid colors. Patterns are too busy and could distract from your face and outfit.

Attaché/Briefcase

Attachés come in various forms. Buy one in a neutral color. If you are on the run all day and need storage, consider a pull attaché.

INVESTMENT SHOPPING

Clothes shopping is a necessity for everyone. The Outfit Option™ Worksheet, combined with investment shopping, will make clothes shopping easier. With your planning or shopping list in hand and your knowledge of fabric, color, and cut, you can make conscientious clothes shopping decisions and choose items that will look great on you and coordinate with the rest of your wardrobe. (You don't have to completely eliminate "nonsense shopping"—going out and buying things just for fun—but try to keep it to a minimum.)

Investment shopping means buying clothes that work with your current wardrobe and give you a ROI (Return On Investment). We all live on different budgets. I am not going to direct you to buy only expensive clothing. However, I do recommend quality clothing. Quality clothing costs a little more, but it holds together better, keeps its color, and wears nicely. When you consider a clothing item, look at its fabric, seams, and top stitching. Loosely woven fabric, uneven seams, and stretched topstitching indicate that a piece is not very well made. If you buy a suit that is not lined (a sign of poor quality) for two hundred dollars, chances are it will fall apart within three months. On the other hand, if you invest in a suit that is lined and costs five hundred dollars, it will last longer and look much better. Five hundred dollars may sound like a lot for a suit, but if you divide the cost by the number of times you will be able to wear it, it is a bargain.

Whenever you go clothes shopping, think of your wardrobe and how garment pieces will work back into it. The Outfit Option™ worksheet helps you make decisions on what you currently need to fill in your wardrobe and what you may want to buy to extend it. If you have a piece that is hard to match, take it with you to the store. Since the lighting in stores tends to be horrible, try on clothes in natural light near doors or windows. If you routinely practice this process, you will no longer need your worksheet, because you will have developed the knack of only buying items that fit with the rest of your wardrobe.

You have now learned to build and plan an Outfit Option™ for your new work style. You have also learned how to enhance your outer appearance so that you project credibility, authority, and reputation and make a lasting impression!

Are you ready to move on to the next element of professional success? As with the first two, esteem and appearance, you must understand, apply, and practice the next element to secure professional success: speaking intelligently.

ELEMENT THREE

Speaking Intelligently

CHAPTER EIGHT

Articulate, Enunciate, and Knowledgeably Communicate

"Speech is a joint game between the talker and listener against the forces of confusion. Unless both make the effort, interpersonal communication is quite hopeless."

—Norbert Weiner,
The Human Use of Human Beings

*Y*ou should communicate intelligently, not in an overbearing or timid way. Communicating intelligently means communicating knowledgeably, meaningfully, and clearly. It does not mean being rude, dismissive, or self-absorbed.

Communication is complex, because it involves at least two people. The quotation above says it all: when two people communicate, they must navigate through differences, obstacles, and biases in order to come to an understanding of a message. The message is the purpose of the communication, whether it is between two or many people. When a conversation is successful, opportunities arise; however, when a message is lost, disrupted, or misunderstood, business relationships can be damaged.

The goal of communication is to send and receive messages that are positive and productive. Workplace communications aren't always positive or productive, but they should be. Criticism is allowed, but it should be constructive. Generations, genders, and people in all positions must understand one another for communication to be productive.

but not all men like just the facts and not all women like colorful stories.

Instead of pointing fingers at each other, men and women need to understand that all individuals have their own verbal and listening characteristics. Understanding these characteristics is the key to harmonious business relationships between genders, generations, and professions.

There is a big difference between listening and hearing. Hearing is just the reaction to vibrations and sounds. But listening is a skill that requires understanding a message and active involvement in the communication process.

How good are your listening skills?

- Do you pay attention when someone is speaking to you?

- Do you actively listen to the speaker?
- Do you drift off when being spoken to?
- Do you only pretend to show interest?
- Do you have another agenda when listening, and interrupt any chance you get?
- Do you get distracted from the person speaking by what is going on around you?

You may think you know how good your listening skills are, but check with a trusted colleague or family member to make sure. An outside perspective may be different from yours, so take their response into consideration.

An active listener is sincerely and genuinely interested in the message the sender wants to deliver. The listener uses her ears, eyes, and body language (more in Chapter Ten). She works to understand how the sender feels, even if she does not agree. The listener waits to respond to the message until she has absorbed it and can respond appropriately. She does not act self-centered or self-absorbed.

Learning the active listening process can be difficult, especially if you are a passive or competitive listener. A passive listener is resigned to listening, but she may pretend to listen or only listen to what she wants to hear. Even if she has an interest in the subject matter, she does not connect with the sender.

The competitive listener has an agenda that must be known. She is self-centered, interrupts, talks about her own experiences, believes she knows more than the speaker, and lets the speaker know that.

Passive Listening

Let's look more closely at the passive listener. At one time or another, most women listen passively. Passive listening may seem harmless, but it's not. It can reflect incompetence, ignorance, and laziness, and it may cause you to miss good opportunities. How? Here are some examples.

Example One

You are in a meeting at work. During the meeting, you look at your PDA and respond to text messages. When you are asked a pointed question, you have no idea how to respond.

You were distracted by your PDA while a team member was speaking, which was inconsiderate and left you unprepared to answer a question. When you try to bluff an answer or evade the question, a sharp leader will know that you have not been listening. Your behavior reflects carelessness and causes you to miss opportunities. Pay attention at meetings and you may get the chance to display your expertise.

Example Two

Your supervisor gives you directions, but you do not pay attention. When it's time to start the task, you have forgotten how you were supposed to do it.

You did not pay attention while a supervisor was giving you directions on how to do something. When you ignore instructions, not only is it disrespectful, you do not know how to do the task. Incompetence can lead to termination. Paying attention shows your initiative to do a good job.

Example Three

You are attending an event after work and a colleague is speaking. You don't listen because she always tells long stories.

When you are asked for your opinion; you have no idea what to say.

You didn't listen to a colleague who really needed your opinion, because the colleague was telling a long story and you got impatient. Impatience is usually detectable and can hurt business relationships. Focus on what is being said.

Train yourself to refocus when you start to get distracted. Otherwise, you may jeopardize your job security.

Competitive Listening

Competitive listening needs to be completely eliminated from your communication. Competitive listening is interrupting and being self-centered in a conversation. It is rude and selfish behavior that can hurt business relationships. Here are a couple of examples:

Example One

You are at lunch with colleagues, and one of them starts a conversation about a recent work event. You interrupt your colleague and tell the group your experience with a similar event.

This is an instance of "one-upping," or trying to trump somebody else's experience with your own. "One-upping" is rude and demonstrates a lack of humility. A proper way to handle this situation is to wait until the person has finished telling his or her story. Then, if asked for your opinion, give it; otherwise, do not offer it.

Example Two

You ask somebody for an opinion, but when the person begins to respond, you interrupt.

You defeated the purpose of the conversation. The reason you asked for an opinion was to get one. When you interrupt, you defeat that purpose. Listen carefully to the person's opinion. As he or she is talking, if you have something to say, remember it or write it down, but do not interrupt. Wait to talk until the other person has finished speaking.

Other factors may also prevent you from active listening. Here are some things that may distract you during a conversation:

1   The room is too hot or too cold.
2   You are outside, at a social event, or in some other place where it is difficult to concentrate.
3   Your mind is filled with personal matters or all the other things you have to do that day.
4   You are simultaneously working at your computer or using another technology device.

5 You think you already know everything there is to know about the conversation.

There will always be interruptions, meetings, and deadlines to distract you at work. But when it's time to listen to somebody else, that should be your first priority. When you need to listen, stop what you are doing. Listening is no less important than the biggest deadline on your schedule. Remove as many distracters as possible to become actively involved in listening.

BECOMING AN ACTIVE LISTENER

> *"Genuine listening means suspending memory, desire and judgment—and for a few moments, at least, existing for the other person."*
>
> —Michael P. Nichols

Active listening is more powerful than verbal communication. You will learn much more by keeping your mouth closed than by being a chatterbox. You can lose valuable information when you control or dominate a conversation.

In college, I was a competitive listener, and I learned a process to improve my listening skills. Since then, I have revised and enhanced the process, and I continually teach it in my seminars and one-on-one consultations. Apply this process to your daily life and reap the benefits.

1   **Stop!** Stop doing whatever you are doing and look up at the person who wants your attention. If the conversation is via telephone, you should also stop whatever else you are doing. If you can't have the conversation right at that moment, pick a time to come back to it later, and when that time comes, *stop*!

2   **Open Ears, Eyes, and Mind and Closed Mouth.** If you are talking to somebody in person, make eye contact.

Element Three: Speaking Intelligently

Keep your ears open and your mind clear and don't interrupt. Focus on the person speaking. Put aside whatever else is in your mind. If you have questions while the other person is speaking, write them down or remember them for later. You do not want to interrupt or accidentally ignore any of the message.

After the person finishes speaking, you need to:

1. **Think:** What was the person saying to you? Why did he or she choose to talk to you?
2. **Evaluate:** Digest the message and keep an open mind. Do not become judgmental.
3. **Process:** Formulate your response. If you have questions, ask them.
4. **Remove ego:** Leave yourself out of the answer as much as necessary. If the

speaker was asking for your opinion,
give it without overshadowing him or
her.

5 **Respond:** Respond to the message,
using eye contact.

By routinely using this process, you will refine
your listening skills and improve your business relationships by showing employers, employees, clients, and potential clients that you
understand and respect what they are trying
to convey.

SENDING A MESSAGE

How do you articulate and communicate your
message? With intelligence! Intelligent communication requires not only good listening skills,
but also good speaking skills. Everybody speaks
differently and has his or her own verbal characteristics, or ways of sending a message.

Element Three: Speaking Intelligently

There are many mediums you can use to send a message. In this section, I am going to concentrate on verbal communication. (Communication via computer is also very important and will be discussed in Chapter Nine.)

Verbal communication has evolved over the years, with new words and slang. It is conducted face to face or via telephone or video conference. When you communicate with intelligence, you can reflect confidence and credibility, secure advancement or employment, resolve problems, increase sales, and build positive business relationships. When you communicate a message, have the background knowledge necessary to relay it effectively.

Everyone has his or her own verbal characteristics. These characteristics include your language style, personality, sound patterns, and background knowledge. Each of these characteristics is critical when, you verbalize a message. You do not want to seem overbearing, aggressive, insincere, or rude.

YOUR VERBAL CHARACTERISTICS

What is your language style?

Language style is how you describe something, make a statement, or ask a question. There is no right or wrong style, but it's interesting to see what your style is.

Visual

- "I see."
- "We see eye to eye on the project."

Auditory

- "I heard the complaint."
- "That sounds like a great idea."

Kinesthetic

- "I felt that budget cut."
- "My gut feeling is . . ."

Abstract

- "Many clients are concerned."

- "The departments are sending in their evaluations."

What is your personality?

Personality is the manner in which you deliver the message. This characteristic is critical because it displays your confidence and tact. When you want to enhance your communication skills, you need to pay close attention to your personality, because it can make you more successful or harm your career. What is your personality?

Aggressive

- You deliver a message in a curt or harsh manner.
- You are overbearing, pretentious, mean, and unprofessional.

Passive

- You deliver a message timidly.
- You are not sure of yourself or the subject matter.

Assertive

- You deliver a message with confidence, civility, and respect.
- You are knowledgeable about your subject matter and audience.

How do you characterize your message?

Characterization is how you "paint" the message you are delivering.

Creative

- A colorful, involved story

To the Point

- Just the facts

You may not exactly fit one of these descriptions, and one is not better than the other. Just keep in mind that when you deliver a message, provide the facts you need to make your point without too much extraneous information. If you know somebody's verbal style is different from yours, try to communicate in his or her style.

What are your sound patterns?

- **Intonation**: The difference between a question and a statement
- **Pitch**: Prominence of the word
- **Volume**: Strength and power of your voice

Your personality in combination with your sound patterns can reflect a message that is different from what you meant to convey. Remember: "It's not what you say, but how you say it." Make sure that your sound patterns reflect your message's importance.

How do you enunciate and articulate your message?

Today's workplace contains a variety of cultures and accents. Speak understandably, in proper

English (or whatever the primary language is at your workplace). If you have an accent that is hard to understand, you may want to invest in language classes. Slang generally has no place in work conversations; it can make you appear unintelligent.

Non-Verbal Communication

Body language is an important part of communication. To enforce your message, look the listener in the eyes. Stand or sit up straight. Lower your shoulders and keep your arms uncrossed and legs together. Do not fidget. When you frown, slump, avoid eye contact, keep your head down, cross your arms, or smirk, you project a negative attitude. (I will talk more about body language in Chapter Ten.)

Do you recognize your verbal characteristics? If you are not sure, ask a trusted colleague or family member. Remember, when you're communicating, the receiver's perception is what matters. If your verbal characteristics are not positive or productive, reevaluate them.

THE MESSAGE

The purpose of verbal communication is to convey a message, but sometimes the message gets lost in translation. Have you ever tried to communicate with someone about a problem in the office, but found that the receiver ignored or dismissed your message? That may have been because you were not articulating the message effectively. Let's see how to convey that your message is important.

The sender in a conversation has an idea of what he or she wants to say. In order for the message to be communicated properly, the sender must encode the message so the receiver can decode it and understand it correctly, as the sender wanted it to be understood. When you communicate, do you know what your message is? If it is too abstract, it may be difficult to understand. Knowing your subject matter is just as important as the way in which you articulate your message. For instance, if you are trying to sell a service or product to a company, research the company and its buying habits and needs. Be able to show the benefits of choosing your product or service. Or if you are interviewing for a job, make sure you do research on the company that's interviewing you. When you communicate with an individual, be aware of how that person verbally communicates and listens. Often, the way a person speaks reflects the way he or she will listen.

When you communicate with an audience, it is harder but not impossible to determine that group's verbal characteristics. Do your research. Start with your contact person. Once you have an idea of his or her communication style, ask about the audience, its demographics, and any other information that the contact person has. Do not ask very personal questions—that will negate your credibility.

Element Three: Speaking Intelligently

If you feel that you are often dismissed or ignored when you convey a message, try this process next time:

1   Have all the background knowledge you need to support your message.
2   Document all your facts.
3   Prepared a plan for how to articulate and deliver your message. Expect questions and prepare for them.
4   Ready yourself for your meeting. Practice eye contact, positive sound patterns, and assertive delivery in front of the mirror.
5   Deliver your message!

Finally, put kindness in your communication. Don't sound as if you are giving people orders. Kindness does not reflect weakness, but respect. Use phrases like "please," "thank you," "may I?", "do you understand?", "excuse me," and "I'm sorry."

If you are assertive and articulate and deliver a message with positive sound patterns and with the receiver in mind, you will enhance yourself as an expert and come across as credible.

Now let's turn to the more modern communicative mediums, in which you are delivering a message without the receiver being able to see you.

CHAPTER NINE

Sharpen Your Electronic Communication Skills

*I*n the last chapter, I explained the importance of verbal communication and how it reflects your intelligence. Over the past two decades, new forms of technology have transformed the way we communicate. Today, methods of communication include e-mails, instant messages, video conferencing, podcasts, blogs, etc. Technological communication, also known as computer-mediated communication, is very important.

Your workday includes both traditional and computer-mediated communication. We are going to look at how you can use different communication mediums in a day's work and how they can affect your bottom line.

TRADITIONAL COMMUNICATION METHODS

Traditional methods of communication are still important in today's workplace. Here are the different types of traditional communication:

1   **Face-to-Face:** This is the most effective form of communication in business. You can send positive messages, give constructive criticism, showcase your company, introduce yourself, lead a meeting, and so on. You can also show true sincerity when you apologize. Do not hide behind technology when a situation demands personal attention.

   When you need to address someone at work, carefully consider the words you use, as well as your body language and tone. Remember, it's not what you say, but how you say it.

For example, say you found an error in a project. You go to the person who made the error and act condescending and overbearing. You humiliate the person and solve nothing.

In face-to-face (and all) conversations, you must conduct yourself with dignity. Remember, you are trying to solve a problem. You should deliver constructive criticism, solving the problem so that it does not happen again. Negativity solves nothing.

2 **Telephone:** The telephone allows you to communicate anytime, anywhere. It allows you to seal a deal, provide information, offer a job, solve a problem, or share an idea instantaneously.

When you talk on the phone, you should enunciate clearly. Answer the phone in a professional tone and listen actively when necessary. If you need to take a message for someone else, be clear and kind and write down the caller's name, telephone number, message, date, and time. If you cannot understand the caller, ask him or her to repeat the message.

3 **Written:** I will discuss written communication further later in this chapter. For now I want to focus on the importance of traditionally written letters and the impact they can have. The handwritten letter should still have a place in your communications.

Handwritten notes are not time-consuming or childish; they can actually make you more successful. Handwritten notes can be a validation on a sticky note telling someone she did a good job; a thank you note telling a new client you appreciate his business;

or a congratulatory note to a business acquaintance. There are many situations in which a handwritten note is more appropriate than a computer-generated letter.

Traditional communication benefits you and those around you. Assuming it is useless may cause you to lose some good opportunities.

ELECTRONIC COMMUNICATION METHODS

Today, you can communicate electronically almost anytime and anywhere. You can talk to your clients from the beach, seal deals while you are on vacation, and hold meetings with your team when all of you are in different places.

With all the ways to communicate nowadays, professionalism sometimes takes a backseat to speed. If you send an e-mail, text, or video message filled with errors, the receiver may misinterpret it. Remember, the goal of positive and productive communication is to send a message that will be decoded as it was intended.

Let's take a look at different types of electronic communication.

Written Electronic Communication

1   **Computer/word processing**: In today's workplace, it is rare to see a typewritten letter. With computers, you can check spelling and grammar and use the thesaurus to find great synonyms. However, some letters are still filled with errors.

   Computer-written letters should transmit your message with intelligence, accuracy, and attention to detail. You are responsible for what you write.

2   **E-mail**: I don't know how we ever communicated without e-mail. It is a vital component of workplace commu-

nication. If you don't know how to use e-mail, you need to learn. E-mail allows you to communicate instantly. You can send e-mails from your computer, PDA, or cell phone. E-mail is vital, and you must treat it that way.

E-mails should be written as professionally as computer-generated letters. They should not be overly casual. Pay attention to grammar, syntax, and spelling. Proofread before sending. Don't send messages that reflect badly on you. Professionalism and good etiquette are essential.

Respond to e-mails no longer than forty-eight hours after receiving the original message. If you get so much e-mail that that is impossible, create a form message that is automatically sent when somebody e-mails you, and say in that message when you will get back to the sender.

It is easy for e-mails to get over-looked during a hectic day, but you must do your best to keep up with your inbox or you may hurt your business relationships.

3 **Instant and text messaging**: These communication methods allow you to send very short messages quickly. In general, you should remember that text and instant messaging are casual forms of communication, to use with co-workers and friends. However, if you have clients who use these methods to communicate with you, you can do the same. Maintain the same sense of professionalism that you would in other forms of communication. Avoid slang and emoticons.

4 **Blogging**: Many organizations and home-based entrepreneurs use blogs to keep their clients and potential clients up-to-date on company business or to share stories and opinions. Blogging is

a great way to give your client bases
an inside glimpse of your organization.
Again, watch your grammar, syntax,
and spelling. Write well in order to
involve readers and entice them to become involved with your company.

5   **E-mail newsletters:** Electronic newsletters are used by many organizations
to communicate with their clients and
bring attention to themselves. Information in newsletters should be interesting and relevant to readers and should
be free of errors.

Visual Electronic
Communication Methods

1   **Web cams:** Web cams allow you to
speak with someone else from your
computer. With Web cams, not only
should your communication be intelligent, your appearance is important.
Make sure you do not look nervous or

bored. Carry on the conversation as you would if the person were right in front of you. Professionalism should be apparent even over a Web cam.

2 **Video conferencing**: Video conferences involve more than two people. Display professionalism as you would in a Web cam conversation. You and your colleagues should represent a well-polished team and should make sure to be respectful to one another and not talk over each other.

3 **Web conferencing**: Web conferencing allows participants in different locations to share presentations. This method of communication can complement video conferencing.

4 **Visual-based telephone calls**: This method allows a telephone call to become a virtual face-to-face meeting. Use my recommendations for traditional face-to-face conversations.

5 **Television:** Television is not a new electronic communication method, but because of the recent invention of HDTV, I have included it in this section. If you present information via television, you must speak with clarity and look polished, or you will negate everything you say.

By the time this book is published, there will probably be new methods of electronic communication. Work on becoming technologically savvy so that you aren't left behind!

COMBINING TRADITIONAL AND ELECTRONIC COMMUNICATION METHODS

Both types of communication are essential components of your path to success. Enhance your image by knowing how to positively represent yourself in a traditional face-to-face meeting, a

Web-based conference, an e-mail, and a written note. You will set yourself above the crowd with your impressive communication skills.

You have learned to believe in yourself, dress appropriately, and communicate with intelligence. Now you are going to learn to behave with pride.

ELEMENT FOUR

Behaving with Pride

CHAPTER TEN

Actions Speak Louder Than Words

*n*on-verbal behavior has a powerful effect and influence on a person's self-image. Your behavior represents your message and your accountability. If you say one thing and do another, you will seem unreliable. If you give a presentation you worked hard on but your body language reflects a lack of confidence, you won't make the sale. Your behavior affects your entire self-image; if you want to be a success, you must act like one.

BODY LANGUAGE

In Chapter Eight, I told you how important non-verbal communication is. However, some women find it difficult to behave assertively; they are either too timid or way too aggressive. My goal for you is to project a confident self-image, both verbally and non-verbally. Here are some aspects of non-verbal communication.

Eye Contact

Eye contact is the most important skill that an assertive and confident woman can possess. Eye contact gives you power; you feel it and project it. When you are talking to somebody, make eye contact the entire time. Here's why:

1 It reflects confidence.
2 It shows that you know and believe in your materials.
3 It reflects credibility.
4 It reflects your interest in your audience.
5 It helps you sell your message.

Here are three steps to enhancing your eye contact skills:

Step 1

- Look at yourself in the mirror and re-peat the self-esteem building statements from Chapter Two.
- Conduct this exercise at least once a day to build eye contact confidence.

Step 2

- Practice eye contact in a comfort-able setting—with family members or friends.

Step 3

- In a supermarket or other public but non-workplace environment, keep your head up. When you speak to someone (probably a stranger), look him or her in the eyes. When you walk by some-one, keep your head up and make eye contact.

■ Building your eye contact skills takes time—practice!

Posture

When you have good posture, you reflect your confidence (and it's good for your bones too!).

As a child, you were probably told to sit or stand up straight. As an adult, it is even more important to have good posture. Sit or stand straight, with your shoulders down and head up. Correct yourself if you start to slump or lower your head. Slouching reflects defeat, nervousness, and lack of self-esteem. (If you have a disability that physically prevents you from displaying good posture, you can project your confidence in other ways.)

Poise

How to sit properly

1 Cross your legs or keep them together.
2 Lean forward slightly.

3 Keep your chin up and your head straight or slightly tilted.

4 Keep your elbows off the table.

How to stand properly

1 Stand up straight.

2 Do not stand with your hands on your hips or cross your arms—this can be perceived as hostile.

Your Face

A smile goes a long way. Unless the situation is really serious, it's okay to smile!

These are just a few techniques you can use to project a self-assured but inviting image. Also, make sure to avoid fidgeting, cracking your knuckles, waving your hands around, chewing gum, or any other distracting or annoying behavior. On and off the job, good body language makes you seem like a team player.

BEHAVIOR

Proud behavior is also reflected in your actions. Back in Chapter Two, I spoke to you about responsibility and accountability. It takes only one missed meeting or unexcused day off to hurt your credibility.

Here are three examples of improper behavior that could hurt your career.

Example One

You have started a new job and are excited. You go into training for one week to learn your job responsibilities. You are on a ninety-day probationary period and at the end you will be evaluated. Your two most important job responsibilities are scheduling appointments and responding to new clients through e-mail. You said in your interview that you could handle many e-mails and multitasking.

Element Four: Behaving with Pride

You start your job and are a bit over-whelmed by all your work. You get behind on e-mails and forget to schedule appointments. You think about telling your supervisor, but don't because you don't want to get in trouble.

At the ninety-day review, you learn that your stay is not going to be extended because you did not perform your job well and did not tell your supervisor when you were having trouble keeping up. Your credibility is lost and so is your job.

Why did you have trouble keeping up with your work?

1 You did not work after hours to get caught up.

2 You talked too much on the job.

3 You were too scared to tell your supervisor that you were getting behind.

4 You were untruthful to your supervisor when she asked how you were doing.

You did not accept responsibility and were not accountable for your actions. In the future, if you feel overwhelmed, tell your supervisor and work together to find a solution. Remember, being honest will get you a long way.

Example Two

You schedule an appointment with a potential client, but you miss the appointment. When the client calls, your assistant reschedules the appointment, but you miss that one too.

The potential client tells you that you have lost his business. You try to make excuses for why you missed the meetings, but the client sees through them.

Why did you lose the client?

1   You missed two appointments.
2   You made excuses to justify your actions.

When you say you are going to do something, do it. Your work schedule is hectic and overwhelming at times. But your clients and potential clients have busy schedules, too. Plus, you never know which client will open new doors for you. You never know whom you are going to meet! When you make appointments, stick to them.

Example Three

You are the senior vice-president of human resources for a multi-million-dollar insurance agency. Four department heads report to you. Two of the department heads are behaving badly. One, whom you have a great relationship with, makes excessive personal calls, and the other, whom you know less well, allows the employees under her to dress inappropriately. To resolve these problems, you meet with each department head separately and handle them differently.

You overlook the first department head's personal calls and clamp down on the second department head's problems with dress code. Soon, people learn about the discrepancy between your solutions to the problems. The president of the company asks to meet with you. You could be reprimanded, lose responsibilities, given a less prestigious position, or even fired.

When you are in a position of leadership, you should treat the people around you as equals. There will be times when you need to reprimand employees, but make sure that your criticism is constructive so that it inspires improvement. Don't allow friendly personal relationships with employees to affect your judgment as the leader. In the office, there is usually not room for personal relationships. Unite your team—don't tear it apart. Finally, and importantly, lead by example.

Element Four: Behaving with Pride

Actions speak louder than words. You may speak eloquently, but if your actions go against what you say, your words mean nothing.

It is easy to make excuses, but you are an adult. You must accept responsibility and expect to be held accountable for your actions. Nobody is perfect; everybody makes mistakes. Instead of running away from them, own them, learn from them, and turn them into opportunities.

Now that we have discussed non-verbal behavior, let's look at the other aspects of behaving with pride.

CHAPTER ELEVEN

Earn Respect, Keep an Open Mind, and Be Kind

*R*espect is earned, not given. When you sincerely value yourself and others, you promote understanding and unity.

EARN RESPECT

Are you respected? Do you value yourself and those around you? Many people want respect but haven't earned it. Some women believe they deserve respect simply because of their age, position, or profession. But you must earn the right to be respected. Let's look at a few examples about the importance of respect.

Example One

You are a doctor. You have been practicing medicine for five years. Your bedside manner has become curt, you have prescribed the wrong medication more than once, and you take advantage of your staff. This type of behavior will dramatically decrease the respect that others have for you, even if you don't lose your title.

Example Two

You work in real estate. You see a colleague struggling with a project. Even though you've finished your work for the day, you don't offer to help her. The next day your supervisor asks you to help a co-worker, but you tell him that that isn't your job. You say that you are busy and give other excuses about why you can't help out. Because of your disinclination to be a team member, you lose the respect of co-workers and supervisors.

Example Three

You have been on the job for a couple of years, and you have always had a good relationship with co-workers and management. However, you start showing up late for work, dressing sloppily, and not putting in overtime when needed. Co-workers start to distance themselves from you, and your relationship with management cools. Why? Your behavior is disrespectful.

In all of these examples, you have seen instances of disrespectful behavior, including:

- Laziness
- Elitism
- Sloppiness
- Complaining
- Lack of initiative
- Disregard for company rules
- Lack of responsibility for actions, decisions, and judgments

There are many ways to earn respect, but personal responsibility is the most important. If you are just starting out in your career, behave responsibly to build respect. If you have lost respect in your line of work, there is no overnight cure, but genuine hard work can help you rebuild your reputation.

Ways to build respect

- Respect yourself first. Make good choices and moral decisions.

Element Four: Behaving with Pride

- Appreciate the job you have. If you are unhappy, do not burn bridges. Keep doing good work at your current job even if you are looking for another.
- Don't take advantage of your position if you are in a leadership role.
- Pitch in and help out even if it's not your job. Helpfulness creates unity in the workplace. When you help others, they will remember it and help you if you need it.
- Show initiative. It may be 5:00 P.M., but if your work is not finished, take five to ten minutes or one to two hours to catch up. If you find that you are always putting in overtime, it may be because you have not organized your workload appropriately.
- Don't gossip about your colleagues.
- Take pride in your work, whether it consists of answering phones, teaching students, or treating patients.

- Inspire employees instead of breaking them down. Demeaning and petty behavior does not motivate your team.
- Eliminate complaining and stop being a tattletale. If you have a serious problem with a co-worker, take it to the appropriate supervisor; otherwise, stop complaining.
- Be trustworthy. Those around you need to know that you are dependable and have their best interests at heart.
- Adhere to company rules, even if you are at the executive level. If you break the rules, it a shows lack of respect for the company and yourself.

When you practice these respectful methods, you will earn the respect that you deserve. There will always be those individuals who cut corners, believing they will climb the ladder of success. But they are bound to fail.

OPEN-MINDEDNESS

You must be open-minded. Open-mindedness means not passing judgment on others. Open-mindedness can be hard to develop, but it must be pursued.

The workplace changes and evolves with the passing of every year. Many people fear change and the unknown. However, change can lead to good things. And it is inevitable. Let's look at a couple of examples about changes in the workplace.

Example One

You work in the accounting department and you know that your company is looking at different accounting software programs. You don't want to change the system you currently use. You explain that it is only three years old and smoothly handles all the applications needed. One day, you learn that management has picked a new program and you will be going into training in about a week. You are very nervous.

Any new process is a little scary. However, you can eliminate much of your fear by being proactive.

- Ask your supervisor about the new program and how it will help you do your job better.
- Ask if the program is hard to learn.
- Tell your supervisor that you are nervous.
- Tell your supervisor that you will keep an open mind when learning the new program.
- When you are in training, put forth your best effort to learn.

Example Two

You are a professor at a large university. You learn that your classroom is going to be used by another professor until a new building is built; then you and your department will move to the new building. When you hear the news, you are very unhappy. You think your classroom is yours and you do not want anyone else using it. You also don't want to move. You feel very defensive. What can you do?

- Although the classroom feels like a second home to you, you need to understand you do not own it.
- Develop a good relationship with the other teacher who will be using your classroom. In a respectful manner, ask him to keep your classroom functional.

- Find another place where you can pro-
  ductively work, if necessary. During the
  building process, go take a look at the
  new building. You will see new furnish-
  ings and state-of-the-art technology
  that will benefit your teaching. You will
  become excited and ready to move.

People are also often close-minded when it comes to judging other people. Unfortunately, women judge other women all the time. Catti-ness at work—or anywhere else—is no good for anybody and will get you nowhere. Let's look at two examples.

Example One

You work closely with three other women and two men. You always eat lunch with two of the other women and one of the men. This creates tension in the office. At lunch, you often gossip about your other co-workers. The branch manager calls

you in and says that your attitude is unacceptable. Why?

- Gossiping about your co-workers is
  cruel and unproductive and makes you
  look bad.
- It's fun to go to lunch with friends, but
  it's mean to leave other people out. At
  lunch time, ask if others want to go.

Example Two

You work at a department store. Most
of your co-workers are your age, but a
much older lady also works with you. You
do nothing to include her and do not talk
to her in the break room. When you are
working on the floor, you avoid her.

- Many generations work with one another, and you need to get used to that.
  You can always learn something from

another person, no matter how old they are.

■ If you genuinely and openly communicate with the older woman, you may be surprised to find that you like her.

The last type of judgmental behavior is judgment of opinions. The right to speak our minds is a great freedom. Everybody has opinions and is entitled to them. You should not push your own opinions onto anybody else; you should respect that people think differently.

Example One

You work in finance. You have a successful method for sealing deals with clients and gaining new clients. Your co-workers recognize your success, but one or two approach you about better ways of doing things. You choose not to listen to what they have to say and tell them that you don't want their suggestions. Over time, they stop talking to you.

- You feel that your co-workers don't have anything valid to say. You need to open your mind. At the very least, listening to them would not have hurt you, and they might have good ideas.
- When you close your mind to opinions or suggestions, you may miss out on opportunities.
- When you do not agree with someone always use the adage, agree to disagree. This stops conflict before it starts.

KINDNESS IN THE WORKPLACE

The third way of behaving with pride is to display kindness in the workplace. Some women believe kindness shows weakness; it does not.

Kindness in the workplace comes in many different forms. You can show kindness on the telephone, in e-mails, when you travel, during presentations, during meetings, and anywhere else.

If you are in a leadership position, your kindness will inspire others to be kind, too. If you are supervised by somebody who is unkind, you don't need to be like them.

Let's look at an example that showcases the importance of kindness.

Example One

You are a small business owner with three full-time employees. Everyone puts in hard work and shows initiative, but you, as the business owner, receive most of the recognition for your company's success. Your busy schedule makes you forget to reward your staff.

Element Four: Behaving with Pride

This is unkind behavior. Everybody deserves recognition for a job well done. No matter how busy you are, you must remember to thank your team for working hard. Take some time, even if it is only a minute, to write notes to your employees telling them that they are doing great work and that you appreciate them.

Behaving with pride means being respectful, open-minded, humble, and kind, not conceited, contemptuous, arrogant, or narcissistic. It is an integral part of the path to success. Your behavior is an unspoken language that you must monitor carefully.

We have covered the fourth and final trait, behaving with pride. You have learned how to be a respected, respectful, and confident woman.

Bringing It All Together

CHAPTER TWELVE

Pull All Four Elements Together and Become a Successful Female Professional

*Y*ou have finished the journey to becoming a reputable, credible, respectable leader in your professional life! Don't you feel empowered? I bet you do! You have learned all the secrets to becoming a successful woman. The road is not easy, but practice and application in your life will be fruitful for you.

Let's take a quick look at how the four elements of self-image complement each other. Turn to earlier chapters if you have forgotten something. There is a lot of information in this book and sometimes it takes reviewing a chapter or two to understand the points.

ELEMENT ONE
POSITIVE SELF-ESTEEM

The foundation of any successful woman is positive self-esteem. Remember these eight aspects of positive self-esteem and apply them to your daily life to build your self-worth:

- Belief in yourself
- Honesty
- Responsibility and accountability
- Aspiration to greater things
- Self-motivation
- Respect for yourself and others
- Graceful acceptance of criticism
- Validation of others

Surround yourself with positive people at work and at home. This will enhance your self-worth.

ELEMENT TWO
A POLISHED APPEARANCE

Your appearance speaks volumes. In Section Two, you learned why your appearance is important on and off the job. Chapters Three through Seven reminded you that your appearance is more than just clothes. It is an updated, age-appropriate style that fits well and includes appropriate accessories and makeup and good hygiene. You learned how to:

- Dress for an audience of one or many
- Develop your own sense of style
- Determine your own body shape
- Understand different types of clothing
- Build an OOWW (Outfit Option™ Work Wardrobe)
- Choose accessories and pay attention to details
- Investment shop

Your appearance in the workplace, whether you work from home or in an office, is a critical aspect of professional success.

ELEMENT THREE
SPEAKING INTELLIGENTLY

Speaking intelligently means speaking knowledgeably, meaningfully, persuasively, and clearly. In Chapters Eight and Nine, you learned how to speak and listen effectively. You also learned how to integrate traditional and electronic communication methods. You learned to:

- Be an active listener.
- Articulate, enunciate, and carefully communicate your message with your listener in mind.
- Develop your message so that it does not get lost in translation.
- Use traditional communication because it carries value and is still very effective.

■ Act professional when using electronic communication forms.

ELEMENT FOUR
BEHAVING WITH PRIDE

Non-verbal behavior is very powerful. In Chapters Ten and Eleven you saw that your behavior must match your verbal message. You also learned that behaving with pride does not mean being arrogant.

You learned how to:

■ Make good eye contact.
■ Use proper posture.
■ Act with poise.
■ Earn respect.
■ Keep an open mind.
■ Use kindness inside and outside the workplace.

If you want to be a success you must act like one.

Self-esteem + a polished appearance + speaking intelligently + behaving with pride = a successful female professional!

If you feel good about yourself, care about the way you look, speak intelligently, and behave with pride, you will possess self-worth.